A NEW PENTECOST

FOR A STARVING WORLD!*

BR. THOMAS VARKEY

The Prophet from Oklahoma City, USA

Potentially the Most Powerful Book Ever Written Since the Bible!

(Because of its huge impact on Practical Christian Living and Discipleship)

---

* Promising eternal hope, divine truth, God's righteousness, perfect peace, and unending joy to everyone!

ISBN Paperback: 979-8-9909519-2-1
         eBook: 979-8-9909519-3-8

For permission requests or to order copies of the book, or for any other requests, please contact the author/publisher via the address below:

Br. Thomas Varkey or
Jesus Army Ministries, Inc.
P. O. Box 350889
Frisco, TX 75035-0889

Printed in the United States of America

DID YOU KNOW?

Did you know that all of us live twice only: a few years here and then forever in the next world?

Did you know that if we miss living for Jesus in our life on this earth by ignoring what the Word of God says about how we can live for Jesus, we will miss the greatest opportunity ever in our life and miss paradise for all eternity in our next life? If you are not convinced of this eternal truth, consider this tragic picture almost always being played out in the lives of almost everyone living on this planet.

Most people work very hard on their job doing what they do for a living, so they can live comfortably in their homes, pay their bills on time, etc. Most of them do all these so that they have enough money left to go on an annual vacation for a week or two of their working years. And they seem to be perfectly happy living this way until tragedy hits them one day, and thus, their life is snatched away from them once and for all—at least that is what they think is the end of their lives!

But Jesus promises infinitely more. He promises us that if we are willing to live our life—we live here on this earth for him—we can live with him like a prince or princess for all eternity for millions and billions upon trillions of years without an end, enjoying the perfect joy and eternal peace. This includes everything that you can think of for being perfectly happy forever and ever according to what we read in Psalm 16:11 and elsewhere in the Bible. In Psalm 16:11, we read: "You will fill me with joy in your presence, with eternal pleasures at your right hand."

If Jesus is promising so much for us, why would we want to settle for the fires of eternal hell, which is what we are going to get after our life here on earth which is so uncertain that not even the next minute is not guaranteed for us here?

<u>Thus says the Prophet (Br. Thomas Varkey):</u>
This is what the SOVEREIGN LORD says:

> **I myself will take a shoot from the very top of a cedar and plants it; I will break off a tender sprig from its topmost shoots and plant it on a high and lofty mountain. On the mountain heights of Israel, I will plant it; it will produce branches and bear fruit and become a splendid cedar. Birds of every kind will nest in it; they will find shelter in the shade of its branches. All the trees of the field will know that the Lord bring down the tall tree and make the low tree grow tall. I dry up the green tree and make the dry tree flourish.**
>
> **I the Lord have spoken, and I will do it. (Ezek. 17:22–24)**

Note: It was through the above passage that the LORD spoke clearly to the author about thirty years ago that he was planning a powerful ministry that will spread into the various parts of the world among Christians and non-Christians alike. Through this ministry, many will come to know and draw close to God. It is this vision that prompted the author to target ten million people to be brought to Christ through this ministry. The LORD has spoken to him that it is not going to be easy, but with the LORD's help, he will achieve it!

Thus says the Prophet (Br. Thomas Varkey):

Thus, declares the Lord, "The house of Israel and the house of Judah have been utterly unfaithful to me, they have lied about the LORD; they said, 'He will do nothing! No harm will come to us; we will never see sword or famine. The prophets are but wind and the word is not in them; So let what they say be done to them.'"

Therefore, this is what the LORD God Almighty says:
"Because the people have spoken these words, I will make
my words in your mouth a fire And these people the wood
it consumes." (Jeremiah 5:14)

(The above words [in italics] were the exact words spoken by the Lord to Jeremiah in the Old Testament period and have now been also given to the prophet to be shared with you.)

Some Remarkable Facts about This Book That You Should Know

This book is not an ordinary book. If you take seriously what this book talks about *being born again,* it will change your life inside out. For example, this book will show you how to live a holy and blameless life, which was the dream that God had about us when he created us. Thus, we read in Ephesians 1:4, "He chose us in him before the creation of the world to be holy and blameless in his sight." Again, in 1 Peter 1:15–16, we read, "Just as he who called you is holy, so be holy in *all you do*; for it is written: 'Be holy, because I am holy.'" And finally, in 2 Corinthians 7:1, we are commanded, "Since we have these promises, dear friends, let us purify ourselves from everything that contaminates body and spirit, perfecting holiness out of reverence for God." In other words, according to God's plan, the very purpose of our life on earth is to **aim to perfect** our holiness to match the holiness of God Himself! This book is the result of a personal experiment that the author conducted lasting for more than 25 years. The author is saying this based on what Jesus told the Pharisees about how the Word of God can change us! Let the author himself tell you how it changed him in his own words.

On October 27, 1997, I heard a Gospel message in which the preacher was narrating an encounter where Jesus told the Pharisees that "to whomever did the Word of God come, they shall be called gods, and that it must and will happen because the Scripture cannot be broken." So I started reading the Word of God devoting every day one to one-and a half hours for the study of the Word of God. It started transforming me so profoundly that I started living differently in ways that would otherwise have been unthinkable before. I started loving others as Christ loved us! For example, on one occasion, I charged my credit card a sum of $67,000 to help one of my distant family members who lost his lease on the place he was doing business. It took me two years to pay off that debt. Paying off was not easy as I had to take out eight other bank loans before I could pay the credit card off. Some of the other "extraordinary deeds of outrageous generosity" that I did can be read in my fifth reason for my writing this book in the first part of the book.

But undoubtedly, the most remarkable of all benefits of *being born again* is the one who is born again can live without sin. How this is made possible by the Holy Spirit is explained in detail in the chapter on the "Benefits of Living According to the Prompting of the Holy Spirit."

But certainly, the most exciting part of this worldwide ministry for which I have written this book is to win over ten million people (about half the population of New York City or about a third of the population of Delhi, India) for Christ, God willing, by the grace of God. I am announcing this upcoming new and humungous ministry project here as an invitation to all who want to join me in this most exciting ministry by organizing and/or participating in the prayer rallies, fasting and praying for this ministry, or by making financial contributions for the expansion of this worldwide ministry.

We read in Psalm 126:5, "Those who sow in tears will reap with songs of joy." I can assure you that one day, Jesus will turn our wailing into dancing (Psalm 30:11). When we reach heaven, our Father in heaven will throw for each one of us the most amazing party in heaven described in Luke 15:22–24, saying to his servants, "Quick! Bring the best robe and put it on him/her. Put a ring on his/ her finger… So, they began to celebrate." Once again, I am confident that God will be with us throughout this worldwide ministry even as we sow the seeds of the Word of God since He has promised me His faithfulness for this worldwide ministry through Ezekiel 17:22–24. Also, in John 14:12, Jesus said, "Anyone who has faith in me will do…even greater things than these, because I am going to the Father." Jesus did not convert ten million souls when He was on this earth! But with His help, we will do it because I have faith in His promise in John 14:12. Our Jesus is a faithful God who keeps ALL *His promises just as He has kept His promise to me that He made twenty-five years ago that "whoever is filled with the Word of God will BOTH become and live like him on this earth."* Praise the Lord, alleluia!

ONE VERY IMPORTANT REASON WHY EVERY CHRISTIAN MUST BE BORN AGAIN! AND TWELVE REASONS FOR WHY EVERY CHRISTIAN MUST SET PRIORITIES IN LIFE!!

THE ONE REASON WHY A CHRISTIAN MUST BE BORN AGAIN!

In Mt. 12:36 Jesus said: "I tell you that men will have to give account on the day of judgment for every careless word they have spoken." If this is so, men MUST also give account for every careless deed they have done while they were on this earth. Before a Christian is born again, ALL his thoughts, words and actions will be unholy and sinful as we read in Rom. 3:10. But when he is born again, not only his words and actions but even his thoughts will be holy. Because according to 1 Jn. 3:9 and 1 Jn. 5:18, a born-again Christian will soon become sinless when he is born again. This is the reason why Jesus said that every Christian MUST BE born again after which his every thought, word and action will be controlled by the Holy Spirit and therefore holy.

THE TWELVE REASONS WHY A CHRISTIAN MUST SET PRIORITIES IN LIFE!!

After everything is said and done, what should our ONLY FOCUS IN LIFE be? If you can comprehend the meaning of the answer to this question from the various passages presented below, you will have a good understanding of what this book, A NEW PENTECOST FOR A STARVING WORLD is all about. This introduction is pretty much an essence of this entire book that will keep your life on track with the message of this book for your entire life. Also, it will scream into your ears whenever you deviate from the path laid out for your life by the Holy Spirit however small that deviation may appear to be! You will begin to feel the influence of the Holy Spirit in your life especially after you have become a born-again Christian after you have gone through the four steps described in this book for becoming a born-again Christian!

Having said that, let me introduce to you the 12 passages in the Word of God which I am presenting here in the order in which they will make the maximum impact in your spiritual life. The passages are:

1. Lk. 17:26-29: Here we read: "Just as it was in the days of Noah, so also will it be in the days of the Son of Man. People were eating, drinking, marrying and being given in marriage up to the day Noah entered the ark. Then the flood came and destroyed them all. It was the same in the days of Lot. People were eating and drinking, buying and selling, planting and building. But the day Lot left Sodom, fire and sulfur rained down from heaven and destroyed them all."

   If we die today for example, the only thing that matters is whether we will be ready for our eternal life! Like in the parable of the five wise virgins and the five foolish ones, if we are focused on getting ready for our next life in eternity, we will have acted wisely in this present life and if not, we will be rejected for all eternity when our bridegroom arrives to take us at a time when we least expect his coming! This is what Jesus is warning us about in this passage in Lk. 17:26-29!

2. Mt. 24:36-39: Here Jesus says: "No one knows about that day or hour, not even the angels in heaven, nor the Son, but only the Father. As it was in the days of Noah, so it will be at the coming of the Son of Man. For in the days before the flood, people were eating and drinking, marrying and giving in marriage, up to the day Noah entered the ark; and they knew nothing about what would happen until the flood came and took them all away. That is how it will be at the coming of the Son of Man."

    Then Jesus continues in Mt. 24:42-44: "Therefore keep watch, because you do not know on what day your Lord will come. But understand this: If the owner of the house had known at what time of night the thief was coming, he would have kept watch and would not have let his house be broken into. So, you also must be ready, because the Son of Man will come at an hour when you do not expect him."

3. Lk. 21:34-36: Here Jesus says: "Be careful, or your hearts will be weighed down with dissipation, drunkenness and the anxieties of life, and that day will close in on you unexpectedly like a trap. For it will come upon all those who live on the face of the whole earth. Be always on the watch, and pray that you may be able to escape all that is about to happen, and that you may be able to stand before the Son of Man."

4. 1 Jn. 5:11-12: Here the Apostle John says: "This is the testimony: God has given us eternal life, and this life is in his Son. He who has the Son has life; he who does not

have the Son of God does not have life." No wonder St. Paul said in Phil. 1:21: "To me, to live is Christ and to die is gain." If we can get hold of eternal life, there is no higher goal in life than that! Paul realized this eternal truth about eternal life and once he did that, that was the ultimate end of his search for God, search for happiness, search for EVERYTHING he wanted in life because when we have eternal life, we have everything!

5. 2 Cor. 11:2-3: Here Paul says: "I am jealous for you with a godly jealousy. I promised you to one husband, to Christ, so that I might present you as a pure virgin to him. But I am afraid that just as Eve was deceived by the serpent's cunning, your minds may somehow be led astray from your sincere and pure devotion to Christ." This must be the ultimate concern for everyone in life. Therefore, since we have reached this goal of getting hold of eternal life, we cannot dig any deeper -- for another goal beyond this one in life. However, we must be constantly vigilant to make sure that the serpent will not lead us astray from this one and only single-most focus of not being led astray by Satan in life.

No wonder the psalmist wrote in Ps. 16:5-8: "LORD, you have assigned me my portion and my cup; you have made my lot secure.
The boundary lines have fallen for me in pleasant places; surely I have a delightful inheritance."
I will praise the LORD, who counsels me;
even at night my heart instructs me.
I have set the LORD always before me.
Because he is at my right hand, I will not be shaken.
Therefore my heart is glad and my tongue rejoices;
my body will also rest secure, because you will not abandon me to the grave.

You will fill me with joy in your presence; with eternal pleasures at your right hand."

6. 2 Pet. 3:12-18: Here Peter tells us: "Beloved, wait for and hasten the coming of the day of God, because of which the heavens will be dissolved in flames and the elements melted by fire. But according to his promise, we await a new heaven and a new earth in which righteousness dwells.

Therefore, beloved, since you await these things, be eager to be found without spot or blemish before him and at peace with him. And consider the patience of our Lord as salvation.
Therefore, beloved, since you are forewarned, be on your guard not to be led into the error of the unprincipled and to fall from your own stability. But grow in grace and in the knowledge of our Lord and savior Jesus Christ."

7. Mt. 5:43-48: Here Mathew tells us: "You have heard that it was said, "Love your neighbor and hate your enemy.' But I tell you: 'Love your enemies and pray for those who persecute you, that you may be sons of your Father in heaven. He causes his sun to rise on the evil and the good and sends rain on the righteous and the unrighteous. If you love those who love you, what reward will you get? Are not even the tax collectors doing that? And if you greet only your brothers, what are you doing more than others? Do not even pagans do that? Be ye perfect, therefore, as your heavenly Father is perfect."

8. Heb. 12:14: Here St. Paul tells us: "Make every effort to live in peace with all men and to be holy; without holiness no one will see the Lord." To be holy, it is necessary

to be at peace with everyone around us at home or outside home. If we are not at peace with others, it means that we have something against them which we should forgive them. If we do not forgive them, Jesus says that His heavenly Father will not forgive us also. Conclusion? We will certainly lose paradise for all eternity!

9. Heb. 12:15: Here St. Paul tells us: "See to it that no one misses the grace of God and that no bitter root grows up to cause trouble and defile many. See that no one is sexually immoral, or is godless like Esau, who for a single meal sold his inheritance rights as the oldest son. Afterward, as you know, when he wanted to inherit this blessing, he was rejected. He could bring about no change of mind, though he sought the blessing with tears."

10. 1 Pet. 1:13-16: Here Peter tells us: "Prepare your minds for action; be self-controlled; set your hope fully on grace to be given you when Jesus Christ is revealed. As obedient children do not conform to the evil desires you had when you lived in ignorance. But just as he who called you is holy, so be holy in all you do; for it is written: "Be holy, because I am holy."

11. 1 Pet. 2:1-3: Here Peter tells us: "Therefore, rid yourselves of all malice and all deceit, hypocrisy, envy, and slander of every kind. Like newborn babies, crave pure spiritual milk, so that by it you may grow up in your salvation, now that you have tasted that the Lord is good." In Jn. 17:19 Jesus prays to the Father: "Sanctify them by the truth; your word is truth." As you sent me into the world, I have sent them into the world. For them I sanctify myself, that they too may be truly sanctified."

12. 2 Pet. 1:5-12: Here Peter tells us: "For this very reason, make every effort to add to your faith goodness; and to goodness, knowledge; and to knowledge; self-control; and to self-control, perseverance; and to perseverance, godliness; and to godliness, brotherly kindness; and to brotherly kindness, love. For if you possess these qualities in increasing measure, they will keep you from being ineffective and unproductive in your knowledge of our Lord Jesus Christ. But if anyone does not have them, he is nearsighted and blind, and has forgotten that he has been cleansed from his past sins. Therefore, be even more eager to make your calling and election sure. For if you do these things, you will never fall, and you will receive a rich welcome into the eternal kingdom of our Lord and Savior Jesus Christ."

Note: This whole book, A NEW PENTECOST FOR A NEW WORLD, is meant to be used by the reader for his daily spiritual workout. Everyday, read at least one of the above 12 passages for your daily meditation. In addition, whenever time allows, read also at least one or more of the 19 chapters from Part B of the book also for your daily meditation. You can rest assured that you will grow spiritually.

But before you go on this daily spiritual workout, make sure that you become a born-again Christian practicing the 4 steps for this as described in Chapter 14 of this book!!

A NEW PENTECOST

FOR A STARVING WORLD!

PART A

The Ten Reasons Why I Wrote This Book

PART A
Contents

Part A

Reason 1

We all need to wake up: Prophets, Priests, Pastors and Everyone Else Included! The truth behind the 'Battle for the Crucifix' has a happy ending – Something we must all know according to Apostle Paul.

Note: in this second edition of my book, A NEW PENTECOS-DT FOR A STARVING WORLD, this Reason #1 has been added to replace the previous Reason #1 after some soul searching and its findings which concluded that very often there is more darkness at the foot of a lighthouse than in the area in front of it although this darker area is closer to the foot of the lighthouse. Let me explain myself.

The reason why I added this reason is the fact that I wanted my readers to know that just as in the case of the Prophet Jonah in the Bible, in my case also I need repentance and reawakening as much as those who listen to my message. This is as true in my case as it was admittedly true in the case of Paul also whose admissions in this area also reflected these truths about himself along with his convictions and fears in these areas.

With that said, let us see what Paul says about himself, which further clarifies this point that our spiritual life is a constant struggle and will continue to be so in the future in the lives of everyone of us as long as we live. We can see such weakness displayed in the lives of the Apostles also, even as Jesus went to pray, only a few feet away from them, after inviting them also to pray along with him during the night that he was going to be betrayed. But they all fell asleep as we read in Lk. 22:45 and therefore Jesus asks them here: "Why are you sleeping?"

In 1 Cor. 9:27 Paul says: "I beat my body and make it my slave so that after I have preached to others, I myself will not be disqualified for the prize." Under these circumstances there is only one totally reliable course that we can take to make sure that we can be truly saved which is to trust in the redemptive work that Jesus has done for us by making the three appearances that he has made/will make – two on earth and one in heaven when he entered heaven to plead on behalf of us to the Father for obtaining for us mercy and forgiveness of sins.

Out of the 2 appearances on earth, the first appearance was to provide purification for the sins of mankind as we read in Hebr. 1:3. The second earthly appearance is yet to come which is going to be at the end of time when he will come to bring salvation for those who, being sinless, will be waiting for his coming to take them with him to heaven as we read in Heb. 9:28.

First time when he came, as we read in Col. 1:20, he also established peace for us with the Father by the shedding his blood on the cross.

In the same way, we read about Jonah also sleeping even as the ship in which he was sailing was almost sinking as it was being tossed around in the storm which was the reason why the captain of the ship asked him why he was sleeping in the middle of all the turbulent storms. I can relate to each of these people who were sleeping when they ought to have been praying to overcome the adversarial conditions facing them. I have often felt that I should have shown more zeal in praying and in my preaching so that I could have been a better model to each of you who are reading my book. This is so very true since the challenge in front of me since I was transformed and became a born-again Christian was to become as closely resembling Jesus as possible. Had I done that, my testimony to the Word of God in Jn. 10:34-35 would have been much more credible to a watching world!

However, it is a fact that after becoming a born-again Christian, I have been able to do some amazing things such as the writing of this book and performing also some acts of outrageous generosity to help others financially some of which are listed in this book! When I say this, I do want to point out that what I have tried to achieve was to become an increasingly and constantly transforming Spirit-filled servant of Christ approaching a level of holiness which would hopefully enable me one day to stand toe to toe with Christ! What has encouraged me to attempt such a fiat is what Jesus says in Lk. 6:40 where Jesus says: "A student is not above his teacher, but everyone who is fully trained will be like his teacher."

The lesson that I learned from my life by modeling myself after Christ to become as closely resembling to Christ as possible is that to achieve anything in our spiritual life, prayer is much more important than anything else! No wonder Jesus said in Jn. 15:5: "Apart from me, you can do nothing." This is also the lesson that we learn from the book of Jonah. Because as we read in Jonah 1 :6, the captain went to Jonah and said to him: "Why are you not praying" (Paraphrased). Get up and call onyour god! Maybe he will take notice of us, and we will not perish." So, Jonah told himthat he was a Hebrew who worshipped the LORD, the God of heaven, who made the sea and the land." He also told him that the reason for all the trouble the ship was facing was that he tried to run away from God because he didn't want to obey God.

When the people of Nineveh heard what he had to say, as we read in Jnh 1:14-16, they cried out to the LORD and greatly feared him and offered a sacrifice to Him and made vows to him. Jonah also prayed to the Lord lying in the belly of the fish as we read in Jnh 2:9. The Lord in return saved the people of Nineveh who exceeded 120,000 in number.

DO I HAVE SOMETHING IN COMMON WITH JONAH?

Like Jonah, I have also asserted myself to convince the Syro-Malabar Church hierarchy not to move the crucifix from the altars of the churches within the Syro-Malabar Catholic Church, one of the two universal churches within the Roman Catholic Church, the other one being the Latin Rite Catholic Church, both under the dominion of the Roman Catholic Church Leader, the Pope. I was very assertive in making them known that it was sacrilegiously wrong to move the Crucifix to make room on the altars of the Syro-Malabar churches for the idolatrous Sliha Cross, often fondly called the Mar Thoma Cross! This was consistent with the teaching of the previous Pope Benedict XVI who said in his book, the *Spirit of Liturgy* that "To move the Crucifix from the center of the altar to the right or the left of the altar was "absurd". On one Sunday morning, with the help of one of the other fellow parishioners of the St. Alphonsa Catholic Church in Coppell, Texas, USA, I replaced the two Sliha Crosses on the two altars of the church with the Crucifixes that I had purchased and readied in advance for this purpose.

Naturally, the then parish priest, Rev. Fr. Sasseril was very upset with what I did and refused to say the Mass until the culprit who placed the Crucifixes on the altars apologized for what he did. I responded to his demand and said to him that "if I had done one thing right in my entire life, it was what I did that morning meaning the replacing of the idolatrous Sliha Crosses with the Crucifixes and that I will never apologize for what I did since it was the right thing to do." He waited for about 10 minutes hoping that I would change my mind and apologize which I didn't. Finally, one of the Committee members apologized on behalf of me and Rev. Fr. Sasseril went on with the Mass after placing the Sliha Crosses back on the two altars where they stood before I replaced them with the Crucifixes. This incident happened on or about May 24, 2010 more than 14 years ago.

Under the above circumstances, what I could do was to pray to God and to the crucified Savior on the Cross which I did asking him to take care of the matter since I was powerless under the above circumstances! I am happy to report that my prayers were heard, slowly but surely though, by the Savior who went to the cross for me and for everyone else currently living on this earth today! Jesus gave me a sure sign that he heard my prayer by removing Rev. Fr. Sasseril from priesthood within a few days from the above incident! The Lord Jesus continues to answer my prayer to this day with many miraculous events which reflect the truth that the Sliha Cross is an idolatrous cross which has caused the Syro Malabar Church to go through many events which have taken away the peace in the entire Syro-Malabar Church like never before in the history of the Syro-Malabar Church! There have also been many violent incidents recently and ever after the introduction of the Sliha Cross within the Syro-Malabar Church when even priests have engaged in physical fights even as they were celebrating the Mass due to the differences of opinion over subjects such as which way the priest should turn while saying the Mass, etc. So many unthinkable incidents such as the head of the Syro-Malabar Church secretly selling most of the major portions of real estate belonging to the Syro-Malabar Church in various locations, and then squandering the money realized through the sale of such properties for personal use by the previous head of the Syro-Malabar Church, etc. Just a few days ago around August 10, 2024 or so, the Pope has expressed his objection regarding the hanging out of the recently defrocked Cardinal of the Syro-Malabar Church in the premises of the headquarters of the Syro-Malabar Church in the State of Kerala. There have also been many threats by the current head of the Syro-Malabar Church who succeeded the previous head of the Syro Malabar Church to defrock bishops and priests who refuse to support the placing of the Sliha Cross on the altars and other such improper and sacrilegious practices which are inconsistent with both the letter and the spirit of the Word of God, etc.

More and more Syro-Malbar Catholics are becoming increasingly convinced that the introduction of the Sliha Cross or the Mar Thoma Cross was a big theological error and a sacrilegious act as it is totally against the Word of God and a creation of man's whims and fancies! Thus, it is becoming increasingly clear that the introduction of the Sliha Cross was a disastrous error in the way the Holy eucharist is to be celebrated both from the perspective of the Word of God and also a total departure from the directives of the Head of the Catholic Church who is the Pope! But based on the disastrous results of the attempts of the Syro-Malabar Church hierarchy for making the Sliha Cross a permanent fixture on the altars of their numerous churches both in India and abroad, we can safely say that the whole attempt to introduce the Sliha Cross and the various paraphernalia which accompany it has been a huge failure and it is a big win for the Crucifix which alone should be adorning the altars of all Catholic Churches in both the universal churches within the Catholic Church namely the Latin Rite Catholic Church and the Syro-Malabar Church! I have every reason to say this emphatically based on how the Lord has answered my prayers as well as the prayers of the more than 99% of the Catholics within the Catholic Church to keep the Sliha Crosses away from the altars of the Syro-Malabar churches!

Thus, in this case, finally we can rejoice that the story of the battle for the Crucifix in the

Syro-Malabar Church has a happy ending based not only on the way that the Lord is protecting the Crucifix because of its huge salvation implications for both the redemption of mankind as well as its theological basis in the Word of God and especially the following 8 verses as follows:

1. Gal. 6:14 where we read Paul saying: "May I never boast except in the cross of our Lord Jesus Christ, through which the world has been crucified to me, and I to the world."

2. 1 Cor. 11:26 where we read: "For whenever you eat this bread and drink this cup, you proclaim the Lord's death until he comes." I truly believe that based on this verse, and since the Sliha Cross has nothing to do with the death of our Lord Jesus Christ and the Cross is inconsistent with the express intention of the Holy Mass mentioned in the Word of God (1 Cor. 11:26 and 1 Cor. 2:2), this man-made cross is a heretical aberration from the Word of God!

3. Jn. 3:14-15 which says: "Just as Moses lifted up the snake in the desert, so the Son of Man must be lifted up, that everyone who believes in him may have eternal life."

4. Lk. 23:40-43 which says: "But the other criminal rebuked him. "Don't you fear God," he said, since you are under the same sentence? We are punished justly, for we are getting what our deeds deserve. But this man has done noth-

ing wrong." Then he said, "Jesus, remember me when you come into your kingdom." Jesus answered him, "I tell you the truth, today, you will bewith me in paradise." No doubt here that this first miracle worked by Jesus hanging on the cross is an affirmation of the salvation power of the Crucifix affirmed by Christ himself which is currently displayed in almost 95% of all the Catholic churches in the world including almost half of the Syro-Malabar Catholic churches and increasing! Moreover, it is consistent with the proclamation made by the late Pope Benedict XVI who said in his book, the Spirit of Liturgy that the crucifix should not be moved from the center of the altar to the right or to the left" much less move it to the side of the sanctuary which has been done in some of the largest churches belonging to the Syro-Malabar Rite.

In Rom. 13:11-12 we read: "And do this, understanding the present time. The hour has come for you to wake up from your slumber, because our salvation is nearer now than when we first believed. The night is nearly over; the day is almost here. So let us set aside the deeds of darkness and put on the armor of light. Let us behave decently as in the daytime, ... clothe yourselves with the Lord Jesus Christ."

And the way we clothe ourselves with the Lord Jesus Christ is by becoming a born-again Christian using the 4 steps that I am sharing with you in the 14th Chapter of this book, A NEW PENTECOST FOR A STARVING WORLD.

According to Rom. 8:9, if anyone has the Spirit of Christ, he will be saved because he belongs to Christ! And everyone who is born again has the Spirit living in him!

In the passage above in Lk. 23:40-43, the criminal who simply told Jesus to remember him when he came into his kingdom was instantly saved for all eternity. This is also an easy and simple way to be saved!

Finally, to those who still go after the Sliha Cross or the so-called Mar Thoma Cross, even after reading all the verses quoted above and the theological arguments made here to establish the authenticity of the Crucifix versus the Sliha Cross, I must ask you the same question that Paul asked the Galatians in the church of Galatia as we read in Gal. 3:1-5. Here Paul asks:

"You foolish Galatians (Syro-Malabar Catholics)! Who has bewitched (deceived) you? Before your very eyes Jesus Christ was clearly portrayed as crucified. Translation: Here Paul is telling the Galatians that if they want to know who Christ is: Look at the crucifix! Any other picture of Jesus is not Jesus Christ. This is the reason also why Paul says in 1 Cor. 2:2: "For I resolved to know nothing while I was with you except Jesus Christ and him crucified."

As the God-designated Prophet from Oklahoma City, USA, and using my God-given prophetic authority in this regard, I am also asking the Syro-Malabar Church hierarchical bishops and priests who are pushing he Sliha Cross down the throats of the innocent Syro Malabar Catholics the same question that Paul is asking the Galatians: "Who has deceived you, fellow Syro-Malabar Catholics? If you want to know who Jesus Christ is: Simply look at the Crucifix. Bring the Crucifix back to the center of the altar where it was before you were deceived by Satan himself and moved the crucifix to the side of the sanctuary! Try to understand the meaning of this verse from 1 Cor. 2:2 in your Bible: "For I resolved to know nothing while I was with you except Jesus Christ and him crucified." For Christ's sake, please, please understand what Paul is telling you! It is not I who is telling you this! I am only affirming what Paul the Apostle says here using the prophetic authority given to me by God through his servant priest, Rev. Fr. Jose Vettiankal more than 30 years ago! Please open your eyes and see that the only way for you to know Christ is by looking at the Crucifix and Crucifix only (1 Cor.2:2)!!

You foolish Galatians! Who has bewitched you? Before your very eyes, Jesus Christ was clearly portrayed as crucified. I would like to learn just one thing from you: Did you receive the Spirit by observing the law, or by believing what you heard? Are you so foolish? After beginning with the Spirit, are you now trying to attain your goal by human effort? Have you suffered so much for nothing – if it really was for nothing? Does God give you his Spirit and work miracles among you because you observe the law, or because you believe what you heard?"

The reason why the Apostle Paul is so obsessed as to call the Galatians 'foolish' was that they insisted on obeying the law instead of putting their faith in God. Also, as we read in Hebr. 11:6, "Without faith, it is impossibles to please God." Another very important eternal truth is that as we read in Hebr. 9:22: the law requires that "without the shedding of blood, there is no forgiveness."

Since the use of the Sliha Cross in the place of the Crucifix in the Syro-Malabar Churches does give an appearance that they are trying to avoid the blood of Jesus which is necessary for the remission of sins as we saw above in Hebr. 9:22 whether it is intended or not!

Intended or not! After all, the only way anyone can be saved from eternal damnation brought on by man's sin is to accept and believe in the blood of Jesus Christ as the only remedy there is for the remission of the sins of mankind. While this is so, getting away from the crucifix and embracing an idolatrous man-made cross such as the Sliha Cross which does not even distantly connect us with the blood of Christ in any way, no doubt, is a sure recipe for separating us from the salvation plan of God for humanity. No wonder Paul called the Galatians foolish for trying to embrace a Jesus far removed from the precious blood that he shed on the cross for the remission of the sins of everyone who wishes to be saved. He was fully convinced that the only way to know Christ was by embracing Jesus Christ as him crucified as he made it very clear in 1 Cor. 2:2.

This was also the reason why Pope Benedict XVI categorically declared that moving the crucifix from the center of the altar to the right or to the left was a foolish thing to do. Therefore, it should never be done by anyone who wants to be saved. This is so because as we read in Hebr. 9:22: "without the shedding of blood, there is no forgiveness" of sins for mankind! Praise the LORD, HALLELUIAH!

Reason 2

Our world is going from bad to worse in all areas such as human relationships, Agape love, morality, and integrity

When we look around us, we see a very bleak condition pretty much all around the world whether it be in morality, human relationships, standards of justice, or righteousness. When we look at people all around us, pretty much in all countries around the world, human kindness and compassion for each other are disappearing, truth is being labeled as "out of style" and irrelevant, and lies are being peddled as virtuous and the only way to embellish our self-serving "happiness," which alone will make us "happy." Grabbing what is important to each one seems to be the primary concern no matter what the social costs may be; getting *what I want* seems to be the only thing that matters to each one all around us! Everyone seems to be interested in getting what he/she wants as though nothing else matters.

Unlike what has been seen in the past, those who sincerely wish well for the betterment of society seem to be becoming less and less in number. From a biblical standpoint, what we read in Ezekiel 37:1–14 seems to be the norm all around us: a heap of worthless remains of a totally meaningless human existence which reminds us of what we may be facing in the not-so-far future, guaranteed to be more toxic to our human values and even to our very existence than the consequences of a fast-deteriorating climate change which we have been witnessing recently. Yes, we are on a fast-track path which is a super highway that will stir up the anger of an infinitely loving and merciful Jesus, who is now weeping with more sobs than the precious drops of blood that He shed while praying to God on behalf of us! Well, let me draw your attention to the bleakness of what we see all around us which is pretty much comparable to the hopeless scene we see described in Ezekiel 37:1–14 in the words of the prophet himself:

> The hand of the Lord was upon me, and he brought me out by the Spirit of the Lord and set me in the middle of a valley; it was full of bones. He led me back and forth among them, and I saw a great many bones on the floor of the valley, bones that were very dry. He asked me, "Son of man, can these bones live?" I said, "O Sovereign Lord, you alone know."
>
> Then he said to me, "Prophesy to these bones and say to them, 'Dry bones, hear the word of the Lord! This is what the Sovereign Lord says to the bones: I will make breath enter you, and you will come to life. I will attach tendons to you and make flesh come upon you and cover you with skin; I will put breath in you, and you will come to life. Then you will know that I am the LORD."

Fortunately, there was a happy ending to this story, and all the bones came back to life and became a living group of people whom God settled in their own land, the land of Israel! Unfortunately, the Lord has not asked me to prophesy to the world that I see around us and thus reinstate all the people living in this world to a state of normalcy. But I feel a sense of obligation and utmost urgency to restore it to a sense of awareness to bring the world back to its conscience and to at least a reasonable level of self-awareness.

For this, I take my marching orders from Proverbs 30:24–25 where God asks us to learn wisdom from the ants which God points out as some of the creatures from whom we human beings can learn wisdom. He tells us to learn from their wisdom which compels them to store up food in summer for the upcoming rainy season and the cold winter that is going to follow. Even though this is only one of the sources of wisdom that the Word of God points out to us, what appeals to me here are a couple of other aspects of their wisdom.

When ants go in a line, when a group of them go in a certain direction, the rest go in the opposite direction. Each of them seems to be embracing the one coming from the opposite direction and telling him that he found some grains of rice in the place it is coming from and that the one he is meeting on the way also can have some of it if he wants to. I am sure this kind of attitude is crucial in our spiritual life if we also want to become wise and live in this world, sharing with one another what we have available in this world and especially the Word of God. But an even greater point of wisdom that we can learn from ants is that oftentimes, we see ants carrying a grain of rice that is probably more than forty or so times heavier than the body weight of the ant itself. The ant seems to tell us that it is carrying this heavy grain of rice not for storing food for himself only for the upcoming raining season or winter but also for the feeding of his other fellow ants! In this day when self-serving interests reign supreme in this senseless world, we all need this kind of wisdom and attitude to carry the burdens of each other in the true spirit of love.

In Galatians 6:1–2 we read, "Brothers, if someone is caught in a sin, you who are spiritual should restore him gently. But watch yourself, or [else] you also may be tempted. Carry each other's burdens, and in this way, you will fulfil the law of Christ." Paul tells us that we have to carry not only our own burdens but also, we have to give a helping hand to others to carry each other's burdens. When we do this, we are fulfilling the law of Christ who paid the penalty for our sins all by Himself, dying on the cross for us all. This serious lesson we can also learn from the ants which are so tiny and fragile but so wise so as to even teach us, who are far more gifted and infinitely more blessed than the ants in respect to the salvation that we alone are called for among all the creatures that we find on earth—my first reason to write this book!

Reason 3

Our church leaders' spiritual
focus needs a makeover:
They need to be Spirit-controlled!

In Philippians 1:21, Paul says, "For to me, to live is Christ and to die is gain." We have to examine the attitude of our church leaders to see if it is even remotely resembling the attitude of Paul as they are leading us spiritually and training us to live a Christ-centered life. But nobody seems to be interested in asking the most important question that needs to be asked of our church leaders as well as each and every fellow Christian that we come across. The primary question that was being asked when one Christian met another Christian in the early church was "Have you received the Holy Spirit?" (Acts 19:2)? Or else, alternatively, the question to be asked was "Do you not realize that Christ Jesus is in you unless, of course, you fail the test?" We consider such a question offensive if it were to be addressed to us on this day and in this age. But this was a routine question to ask in the early church as we observe from the above two passages. As somebody accurately stated, "The sign of maturity is asking the right questions and questioning the wrong answers."

Now the question is, how critical was this question to ask a Christian living according to Jesus's commands? Jesus said to Nicodemus during His conversation with him, "I tell you the truth, no one can enter the kingdom of God unless he is born of water and of the Spirit" (John 3:5). If we analyze the two questions that the apostles and particularly Paul asked every Christian that he came across, they were paraphrased versions of Acts 19:2 or 2 Corinthians 13:5. But unfortunately, nowadays, to ask this question to our fellow Christians is not only unusual but also offensive. Where did we go wrong that caused us to discontinue asking our fellow Christians this absolutely necessary question? How did we fall off the wagon and put aside this extremely important practice that the early Christians considered so vitally important as to consider this a litmus test question to determine whether a Christian was genuinely a Christian or not? The answer is that slowly, they gave less and less importance to the need to be *born again*, which Jesus had told them was absolutely necessary to enter the kingdom of heaven.

But then one thing led to another and the leaders among the early Christians unknowingly put themselves into a corner and gradually but surely set aside the practice of imparting the Holy Spirit by laying hands on Christians who were not born again. It is absolutely necessary to reinstate this practice which was so commonly prevalent in the early church! This was certainly the greatest deception that Satan used to trick the church and cause it to drop the most solemn practice of "making disciples of all nations," a reality wherever they went with the message of the gospel.

Unfortunately, when this happened, the church fell from grace like a rock, and she became carnal and unholy. For example, the church leaders lost their perspective on what is important not only in their Christian life but also in their Christian worship. An example of the church leaders losing their perspective on what is important in their Christian worship is that in some Christian denominations like the Syro-Malabar Church segment of the Catholic church, the crucifix was relegated to the side of the sanctuary from its center where it occupied its rightful place for centuries and centuries after the church was born. Fortunately, the crucifix is still in the center of the sanctuary in the Latin rite churches. This, in spite of the fact that *Jesus clearly commanded in John 3:14–15, "Just as Moses lifted up the snake in the desert, so the Son of Man* **MUST BE LIFTED UP,** *that everyone who believes in him may have eternal life."*

The crucifix in our Christian worship is to take the central location of the place of worship that the image of the snake erected on a pole occu-

pied when Moses erected the image of the snake for healing the Israelites, who got bitten by the snake when they murmured against Moses and God. **Thus, the most crucial element in Christian worship ceased to be a part of the Christian worship**. Thus, worship **was *downgraded by the replacement of one of the two crucial elements of worship, namely the crucifix,* with a man-made symbol such as the Mar Thoma Cross. The other crucial element, of course, is the Holy Eucharist,** which also is increasingly oftentimes being moved to the side of the sanctuary in the Syro-Malabar churches by the same Syro-Malabar Church leaders! As the God-appointed servant of God, the Prophet from Oklahoma City, USA, *I rebuke this action on the part of the Syro-Malabar Church leaders responsible for this action! I beg you: please, please follow the leader of the Catholic church, the Pope, and the example in the Catholic churches in the Latin rite, and move the crucifix back to the center of the altar if it is not already in the center of the altar!*

As a servant of God, I could not say this in any stronger language! Otherwise, you are insulting Christ who sits on the throne in heaven (Rev. 4:6, 5:6). As a humble servant of Christ who is our Lord, I cannot say in any stronger language that **we cannot move the central location of the crucifix by moving it to the right or the left of the altar any more than move His heavenly throne to the side or a corner of the dwelling place of God** (Rev. 4:6, 5:6). The presently ongoing wide rift in the Syro-Malabar Church is an evidence of the anger of God for this horrible action that has been taken within the Syro-Malabar churches! By this terrible action, the Syro-Malabar Church has altered the design of our place of Catholic worship in such a way that it no longer resembles the worship of God that goes on in heaven (Rev. 4:6–8). This is so because we read in Revelation 4:6, **"Also before the throne there was what looked like a sea of glass, clear as crystal. *In the center*, around the throne, were four living creatures, and they were covered with eyes, in front and in back." Notice the words *in the center.* When we move the crucifix to the side of the sanctuary, we are changing our *worship model* in such a way that it *no longer resembles* the *worship model* that CURRENTLY EXISTS AND WILL ALWAYS EXIST in heaven! This is so wrong!**

In Luke 14:8–11, Jesus talks about what we believers are to do when we are invited for a wedding feast. Here we read: In Luke 14:8–11, Jesus talks about what we believers are to do when we are invited for a wedding feast. Here we read:

> When someone invites you to a wedding feast, do not take the place of honor, for a person more distinguished than you may have been invited. If so, the host who invited both of you will come and say to you, 'Give this man your seat.' Then, humiliated, you will have to take the least important place. But when you are invited, take the lowest place, so that when your host comes, he will say to you, 'Friend, move up to a better place.' Then you will be honored in the presence of all your fellow guests. For everyone who exalts himself will be humbled, and he who humbles himself will be exalted.

By moving the crucifix to the side of the sanctuary, what have our Syro-Malabar Church leaders done to Christ Himself who is the bridegroom at the wedding feast? They have denied him even the least important seat at the banquet! They have sent Him out of the banquet hall to a side room. When this kind of humiliation is being done to the bridegroom, aren't we putting Him through the worst humiliation that we can put Him through? There is no doubt that this is what we are doing to Jesus with the crucifix, which Jesus has said should be at the center of worship in our places of worship so we can not only worship Him but also obtain our eternal salvation, which depends on our looking at His image and repenting of our sins (John 3:14–15)!

If we do not correct this mistake as soon as possible by bringing the crucifix back to the center of the altar where it takes its honorable place as it is being done in more than 99.5 percent of the churches in the Catholic church, we will be severely punished by the bridegroom at the wedding feast who is Jesus Himself! Yes, in the name of the bridegroom, who is and should rightfully be at the center of every worship and every Holy Mass which is the wedding feast where we share the "breaking of the bread," as the prophet of God, I rebuke everyone who attempts to move the crucifix from the center of the altar—before the Syro-Malabar Church turns into a big ZERO!

In this regard, we should listen to Jesus and Pope Benedict XVI who, in no uncertain terms, has promulgated that "the Crucifix should not be moved from the center of the altar to the right or the left" in his book titled *The Spirit of Liturgy*. Such a replacement has made our ***worship model*** **inconsistent with the *worship model* that exists in heaven as it is described in Revelation 5:12 where we read, "Worthy is the Lamb, who was slain, to receive power and wealth and wisdom and strength and honor and glory and praise."** If we look at Revelation 5:6–10, we can see where the slain Lamb is standing; **He is "standing in the center of the throne,"** encircled by the four living creatures and the elders. He had seven horns and seven eyes, which are the seven spirits of God sent out into all the earth. He came and took the scroll from the right hand of Him who sat on the throne. And when He had taken it, the four living creatures and the twenty-four elders fell down before the Lamb. Each one had a harp, and they were holding golden bowls full of incense, which are the prayers of the saints. And they sang a new song:

> *You are worthy to take the scroll and to open its seals, because you were slain, and with your blood you purchased men for God from every tribe and language and people and nation. You have made them to be a kingdom and priests to serve our God, and they will reign on the earth.*

Notice here that the theme of the new song or the object of worship according to *Revelation 5:9 is the slain Lamb who is*

none other than Jesus Christ. Notice also that when the Israelites murmured against God and Moses, **the image of the snake was the means by which they got saved from the snakebites. This was so according to God's instruction in Numbers 21:8. In other words, the salvation of those who sinned against God and Moses depended on "looking at the snake on the pole just once." In John 3:14–15, Jesus Himself said that the image of the Son of Man must also be erected (on the cross), which would then be the means by which we are to be saved (from the snakebites of Satan who is described as *the great dragon* in Rev. 12:9). Thus, today, the image of the Son of Man should also be at the center of our worship and at the center of our repentance.**

In Numbers 21:8, Moses interceded for the Israelites, who sinned against God when they repented and looked at the image of the snake on the pole that was erected for their life being saved from snakebites. In the same way today, Jesus is interceding for the salvation of those who look at His image repenting of their sins from the bites inflicted by Satan, who is described as the snake not only in the Old Testament but also in the New Testament (Rev. 12:3). But for this the image of the slain Lamb should be at the center of their worship as Jesus Himself had instructed us to do according to John 3:14–15 when He was living on this earth.

Thus, according to Jesus, our worship model should have the crucifix on which His image is erected. This way, both in heaven and on earth, it is God's will that Christ, who is our slain Lamb, should be at the center of our worship not only spiritually but also figuratively by having the crucifix at the center of our worship because Jesus Himself had asked us to do it in John 3:14–15. Unfortunately, there are arguments against this in certain segments of the Catholic church such as the Syro-Malabar Church as well as in other denominations. According to the written Word of God and as illustrated above, this is an argument raised against the written Word of God and is therefore a huge mistake that should be corrected as early as possible.

Under these circumstances, there is no time as urgent as this when the church of Jesus Christ is in need of a second Pentecost, which I am now announcing through this book. As I have stated elsewhere in this book, I am convinced that the times we are living in are extraordinary indeed. As we read elsewhere in James 5:9, "The Judge is standing at the door!" And I am once again convinced that I have received *prophetic status* from the Lord for such a time as this (Esther 4:14)! To drive home to you the urgency of the day, I would like to inform you of another message which the Lord has put into my mouth to announce to you (once again handed down to me years ago by my spiritual mentor, Rev. Jose Vettiankal), which is taken from the book of Jeremiah, more specifically from Jeremiah 5:14 which states, "Therefore, this is what the Lord God Almighty says: 'Because the people have spoken these words, I will make my words in your mouth a fire and these people the wood it consumes.'" And thus, the urgency here is clear; this is the second reason why I am writing this book.

Reason 4

Why is God sending all these viruses? It is to convince us of our dire need to "be born again."

Believe it or not, this outbreak of the coronavirus is for the greater glory of God. Having said that, let me address what is the cause of it and the remedy and course of action we are to take.

The causes:

a. The cause can be found in Hosea 4:1–3 where God says, "Hear the Word of the Lord, you Israelites, because the Lord has a charge to bring against you who live in the land: There is no faithfulness, no love, no acknowledgement of God in the land… Because of this the land mourns, and all who live in it waste away." This applies to us also in this time and at this hour. Let us examine one of these charges: do we really love God? In John 14:23–24, Jesus says, "If anyone loves me, he will obey my teaching… He who does not love me, will not obey my teaching."

   i. In Matthew 5:17–18, again Jesus says, "I have not come to abolish the Law or the Prophets, but to fulfill them. I tell you the truth, until heaven and earth disappear, not the smallest stroke of a pen will by any means disappear from the law until everything is accomplished." Therefore, it is clear that Jesus let all the laws that came through Moses and the prophets remain intact except those few which He modified like the laws that applied to adultery (Matthew 5:28) and loving our enemies (Luke 6:27, 29). If this is so, we should ask ourselves the following questions.

ii.   In Psalm 100:4, we read, "Enter his courts with thanksgiving and his courts with praise." Why are we then not entering the gates of our churches singing psalms of praise and thanksgiving? The Jews used to chant psalms and thanksgiving songs whenever they climbed the mountain upon which the Jerusalem temple was perched. That is how the psalms from 120 through 134 were called songs of ascents. If the Jews chanted these whenever they ascended the Jerusalem temple, we should also do it since Jesus says in Matthew 5:20, "I tell you that unless your righteousness surpasses that of the pharisees and the teachers of the law, you will certainly not enter the kingdom of heaven."

iii.   In Exodus 20:4–5 and Deuteronomy 5:8–9, we read the second of the Ten Commandments: "You shall not make for yourself an idol in the form of anything in heaven above or on the earth beneath or in the waters below. You shall not bow down to them or worship them." Jesus has not in any way modified this second commandment nor authorized anyone to make any kind of changes to this commandment. Then why are we having so many statues of various saints and others in our churches?

iv.   In John 3:14, Jesus says, "Just as Moses lifted up the snake in the desert, so the Son of Man must be lifted up, that anyone who believes in Him may have eternal life." Here, Jesus says that the image of Himself erected on a pole must be lifted up so that we can look at His image and be saved eternally. His image was to be used much in the same way as Moses lifted up the snake and thus saved the Israelites bitten by snakes by looking at the bronze snake set up by Moses (Num. 21:8–9). We have not done what He asked us here to do after His death: to raise up the crucifix in our places of worship. Thus, to quote Romans 1:22, "Claiming to be wise, they became fools" has literally come true in our places of worship. By no means is this an exhaustive list of the commandments of God that we disobey! Therefore, as your God-appointed messenger, I would like to remind you that the way to escape the coronavirus, and all other viruses, is to obey the Word of God when it comes to our worship and our repentance. In our worship, we need to display the crucifix just as Moses displayed the image of the snake to revive those who were dying from the snakebites that tortured or killed those who complained against God and Moses during the Exodus. In our repentance, we need to look at the crucifix with faith and thus get remission from all our sins, which are nothing but the smite of Satan and the devil!

v. We have to correct the theological errors that we have been making in the above areas (a to c). Until then, we are in violation of God's commandments, and the pandemics and viruses are nothing but the expression of God's anger caused by our gross violations of His commandments as we see above.

vi. Remember to obey the greatest commandment Jesus has given us, which is found in Matthew 22:37: "Love the Lord your God with all your heart and with all your soul and with all your mind." Give Jesus the first priority in our lives as we are commanded to do in Revelation 2:4 since Jesus is our "first love."

I can go on and on and list many other violations of God's commands and commandments, which displease God in our everyday life. We have to repent for these sins and must stop committing each and every one of them. However, there is an easier way and a shortcut to escape the worry from all the lapses in our obedience and every failure that we may experience as long as we try our best to obey God in everything He asks us to do; AND THEN, DO ALSO THE FOLLOWING: **JUST BECOME A BORN-AGAIN CHRISTIAN.**

This is a shortcut that Jesus won for us by His death on the cross!

This shortcut works even if you theoretically break all the above commandments!

Because according to 1 John 3:9, a born-again Christian cannot sin—well, pretty much. Much more details on how this is made possible by the death of Christ on the cross will be covered under the "Four Steps to Become a Born-again Christian."

Reason 5

Use the theology of being
born-again as an evangelization tool!

In Acts 1:8, Jesus, before ascending to heaven after His resurrection, instructed the apostles to wait in Jerusalem until they received the Holy Spirit whom the Father had promised and thus be baptized with the Holy Spirit. He further told them that when they receive power when the Holy Spirit came on them, "they will be His witnesses in Jerusalem and in all Judea, Samaria and to the ends of the earth."

But after a few weeks and months after they received the Holy Spirit and preached Christ in a few places, they sort of slowed down in their witnessing act and stayed back in Jerusalem and the surrounding areas. After Stephen was stoned to death, the disciples were more afraid to go beyond the boundaries of Jerusalem to witness to Christ and His gospel. Therefore, as we read in Acts 8:1, God sent "a great persecution against the Church in Jerusalem and all except the Apostles were scattered throughout Judea and Samaria." This was a plan of God to disperse the apostles and disciples far and wide so that the gospel would spread throughout the world "and to the ends of the earth."

I truly believe that the ongoing pandemics like COVID-19 and monkeypox are also God's way of forcing the people of God to *go* far and beyond their comfort zones to be witnesses to Christ and His gospel. Certainly, God is inviting us to pray for the evangelization of the world through *prayer and fasting*. We read in 2 Chronicles 7:14, "If my people, who are called by my name, will humble themselves and pray and seek my face and turn from their wicked ways, then will I hear from heaven and will forgive their sin and will heal their land. Now my eyes will be open and my ears attentive to the prayer offered in this place…" Again, in Jeremiah 33:3, God asks us to "call unto him and he promises us that he will answer."

Yes, brothers and sisters in Christ, this is the time to get out of our comfort zones and pray and call upon the name of the Lord and spread the gospel. This is the time we need to have the attitude of Paul who said in Acts 20:24, "I consider my life worth nothing to me, if only I may finish the race and complete the task the Lord Jesus has given me—the task of testifying to the gospel of God's grace." Just remember: this is harvest time. Therefore, we need to get out of all our comfort zones and call upon the name of the Lord! We need to pray in tongues, pray with our heads, and pray in Spirit! We need to pray by dancing as David did in front of the ark! We need to pray all the time as we read in 1 Thessalonians 5:16–18, "Be joyful always; pray continually; give thanks in all circumstances, for this is God's will for you in Christ Jesus."

In Ephesians 1:4–10, we read:

> He chose us in Him before the creation of the world to be holy and blameless in his sight. In love He predestined us to be adopted as his sons through Jesus Christ, in accordance with His pleasure and will—to the praise of His glorious grace, which He has freely given us in the One He loves. In Him we have redemption through His blood, the forgiveness of sins, in accordance with the riches of God's **grace that He lavished on us** with all wisdom and understanding. And He made known to us the mystery of His will according to His good pleasure, which He purposed in Christ, to be put into effect when the times will have reached their fulfillment—to bring all

things in heaven and on earth together under one
head, even Christ.

Yes, Jesus lavished an indescribable amount of grace on us! Now it is our turn to drown Him with our praises and our worship for His infinite goodness which He lavished on us in so many numerous ways! As part of these various forms of prayer, we need to conduct prayer rallies in front of churches and other places of worship as well as distribute tracks that carry gospel messages for spreading the gospel and the knowledge about the four-step way on how a Christian can be born again to ensure our eternal salvation.

It is time for us to upgrade our prayers and their quality and quantity along with our worship and praises we heap up on Him! Our prayers should be upgraded in five different ways:

a. We should pray regularly and always as we read in 1 Thessalonians 5:17.

b. We should pray about everything. In Galatians 6:2 we read, "Carry each other's burdens, and in this way, you will fulfill the law of Christ." This is one way we can be another Christ in this world and carry others' burdens and help them tremendously and almost infinitely as Christ!

c. Pray intelligently. Our prayer should be modeled after the Lord's Prayer, covering all the bases and putting priorities in their proper order as Christ showed us in the Lord's Prayer. Spreading His kingdom on earth should be the highest priority in our lives, as it is reflected in the Lord's Prayer right from the start!

d. Our prayer should not be selfish. We should pray for others much more than for ourselves! We should carry others' burdens in our prayers. This we learn from the way Jesus prayed while He was on this earth. He never prayed for anything for Himself. On the other hand, all His prayers were for His disciples and those who approached Him with various requests such as healing of diseases and for raising their dear ones who had died, etc.

e. Finally, pray confidently. Our confidence is that He will refine our prayer intentions to leave out our prayers for things that are not important and replace them with those that are vital and absolutely essential. The evidence that God does this is found in Romans 8:26–27 where we read, "We do not know what we ought to pray for, but the Spirit himself intercedes for us with groans that words cannot express. And He who searches our hearts knows the mind of the Spirit because the Spirit intercedes for the saints in accordance with God's will."

Reason 6

**Use this book to testify to the truth
that all the promises in the
Word of God are 100 percent trustworthy.**

This I understood from 2 Corinthians 1:20 which says, "For no matter how many promises God has made, they are 'Yes' in Christ. And so, through Him the "Amen" is spoken by us to the glory of God." In this book, I have described how I was absolutely fascinated when I came across the word of God in John 10:34–35 which says, "Jesus answered them, "Is it not written in your Law, 'I have said you are gods'? If He called them 'gods,' to whom the word of God came—and the Scripture cannot be broken…" It was on October 27, 1997, when I read this passage and was overwhelmed by what it says! Here, the context is that the Jews took stones to stone Jesus when He claimed that He was the Son of God. Even though the Jews were looking upon Him as the carpenter's son, the truth was that He came from God as evidenced by the miraculous birth He had following the announcement of the angel Gabriel to Mary, His mother, and the absolutely unusual events that occurred upon His birth in Bethlehem, etc. In the history of mankind, to this day, there has never been a child born when a star appeared above the house where the child was born, angels sang Christmas carols upon its birth, etc. Therefore, for us who are reading all these details about the birth of Jesus in hindsight, we have absolutely no reason to doubt that Jesus was the Son of God even though He was born in that manger in Bethlehem two thousand plus years ago!

But if you are like me, you will be a little taken back if and when Jesus said what He said in the passage above in John 10:34–35. So I could not believe it at that time. But now, I am absolutely certain that it is not only possible but it is absolutely certain. But I am totally convinced that God's promises are absolutely trustworthy based on my own experience! I may not have manifested the full impact of having been totally remade in the nature and essence of Jesus Himself, but due to the conviction that I have after studying the Bible for twenty-five long years, I am convinced that for the rest of my life, I will pretty much radiate the character and goodness of Jesus Himself, at least in the eyes of God if not in the eyes of the people of this world! I know that I am not what I used to be and so do those who knew me twenty-five years ago and know me now as I am today.

Just to give you a couple more examples of how the Word of God has changed me over the years, I like to share a couple of incidents as a testimony to the truth of what I am saying here. When my two daughters were growing up and going to school, an incident happened about which I am not at all proud now, and I would not have done it in a million years if I were the man that I am now. What happened was that one day when my family was living in Chicago and I was dressing up my two girls for school, I got really mad at them because when I dress up one, the other daughter would take off the mittens from her hands to cuddle the hamsters and their babies, which were their pets at that time! This happened a couple of times, and it was getting late to take them to school. I believe the girls were six and seven in age. I got so mad at them that I flushed the baby hamsters in the toilet—not just one or two of the babies but all five of them! Then once, my second daughter was spending a lot of time playing with her baby doll, I threw that doll against the carpet in the living room; that doll got decapitated, with its head landing a few feet from the rest of the body.

How I changed: a few years went by after I started filling my heart and mind with the Word of God! Once, I was driving to Nashville, Tennessee, where my second daughter studied at Vanderbilt University. I was driving alone by myself from Mesquite, Texas where I was living at that time. I was almost crossing the boundary of

Mesquite when I saw a homeless man stretching his hands toward me for a ride as I was driving at sixty-five miles per hour and passed him. I could not stop in time to stop the car close enough to help him. But as soon as I passed him, I stopped on the side of the road and waited for him to catch up with me as I waved to him to walk toward me. It is not even the least desire on my part to brag about myself as I am describing this incident. All I am trying to portray is how the Word of God changed me almost totally!

As I have always done every day without exception even for a single day since October 27, 1997, I have spent an hour to an hour and a half indulging in the meditation on the Word of God or reading it or praying about it! It has transformed me, I would say, to such an extent that it has pretty much made me such a character and personality that twenty years ago I could not have even imagined!

To finish the story of my giving a ride to the homeless man, I took my friend into my car, offered him some of the food I had taken with me for snacking on my way to Nashville, and dropped him off in Texarkana, which is about eighty miles from Mesquite, Texas. I shared with him some passages from the Bible and told him how much Jesus loves us all. When we reached Texarkana, I dropped him off there after giving him a $10 bill to buy some food or to use it however he saw fit.

The second extraordinary act of "outrageous generosity" that I referred to in the "About the Book" section, without including it there, is that while I am currently living in a small house, I have given away enough money to other family members of mine, including members who are not even part of my immediate family. This was done outright without expecting it back. What makes it outrageously generous is that as part of this generous deed, I gave away every penny that I received as part of the dowry money that I got when I got married even though I had not earned even a single rupee to claim as my own. And that too, my wife and I had no house to call our own. I did all these generous donations relying on the faithfulness of God, just like the outrageous credit card loan I took out to help a distant family member of mine. What gave me courage to do such deeds was my faith in the promises of God—more specifically what we read in Proverbs 19:17: "He who is kind to the poor lends to the LORD, and he will reward him for what he has done."

Since then, the next question is, Did the LORD reward me? And the answer is a whopping *yes*. Without going into details, let me tell you that as a result of my taking risks to help others and also spending many sleepless nights, especially when I had to pay off my credit card debt, my faith was greatly boosted, and I have been totally amazed at the faithfulness of the LORD in keeping His promises.

I have several more similar anecdotes to narrate from my life that speak to the tremendous change I have undergone due to my devotion to the Word of God. But I'm sure you get the gist of what I am trying to say here. I am convinced with absolute certainty that what the Word of God says in John 10:34–35 will happen and MUST happen because God said it. I would challenge anyone to take up this challenge for themselves and become like Christ if they are curious and want to give it a try! I am guaranteeing it not because of any magical wand I possess but because the Word of God is absolutely guaranteed to come to pass that you can take it to the bank with 100 percent confidence!

If I were to give you an assurance about the Word of God, which is anything less than what I am giving you here, that the word of God will come to pass as it is written in the Word of God, I will be doing a disservice to the Word of God! This is true about the Word of God no matter how discouraging or impossible the circumstances may appear to be. You can see an example of this from the life of Joseph, the son of Jacob as it is described starting from Genesis 29:10 to the end of the last chapter of Genesis 50.

Reason 7

I think God has given me almost the same zeal as Paul had for spreading the gospel. But one thing God gave me which he didn't give even to Paul!

I admire Paul more than any other apostle of Jesus. He had more insight into the Word of God so as to be able to write fourteen Epistles many more than the apostle John who, I believe, has written more New Testament books than anyone else except Paul. By the mighty grace of God, I was given a special gift that even the above two did not receive. It is the four-step formula on how a child of God can be *born again*. I wondered why God chose to give me this knowledge of the four-step formula which, I am sure, will help many in their spiritual journey and growth and lead them to spiritual transformation so as to "be filled to the measure of all the fullness of God" (Eph. 3:19).

I found no reason for this. However, I have two guesses. One is that God honors the one who honors or seeks to honor Him. Thus, we read in 1 Samuel 2:30, "Those who honor me I will honor, but those who despise me will be disdained." As I said in my reason number 5 to write this book, in 2 Corinthians 1:20, Paul says, "For no matter how many promises God has made, they are "Yes" in Christ. And so, through him the 'Amen' is spoken by us to the glory of God." When I made an earnest effort to reveal the magnificent glory of the gospel to honor Him and Jesus Christ, who is the written Word of God incarnate, God honored me much more than I honored Him. **I**

was first overwhelmed by this kind of enormous generosity on the part of God. But then, I noticed that this is rather typical of God and His Son, Jesus Christ!

Let me give you two examples for illustrating how amazingly generous God is toward those who dare to do something out of the ordinary for the greater glory of God, one from the Old Testament and another from the New Testament. In the Old Testament example, we read about King David's burning desire to build a temple for God, and he talks about it passionately to Nathan the prophet in 2 Samuel 7:2–16. David says to Nathan:

> "Here I am, living in a palace of cedar, while the ark of God remains in a tent." Nathan replied to the king, "Whatever you have in mind, go ahead and do it, for the Lord is with you." That night the word of the Lord came to Nathan, saying: Go and tell my servant David, 'This is what the Lord says: Are you the one to build me a house to dwell in? I have not dwelt in a house from the day I brought the Israelites up out of Egypt to this day. I have been moving from place to place with a tent as my dwelling. Wherever I have moved with the Israelites, did I ever say to any of their rulers whom I commanded to shepherd my people Israel, "Why have you not built me a house of cedar?"'

> "Now then, tell my servant David, 'This **is what the LORD Almighty says: I took you from the pasture and from following the flock to be ruler over my people Israel. I have been with you wherever you have gone, and I have cut off all your enemies of the greatest men of the earth. And I will provide a place for my people Israel and will plant them so that they**

can have a home of their own and no longer be disturbed. Wicked people will not oppress them anymore, as they did at the beginning and have done ever since the time, I appointed leaders over my people Israel. I will also give you rest from all your enemies… Your house and your kingdom will endure forever before me; your throne will be established for ever.'"

"'The Lord declares to you that the Lord himself will establish a house for you: When your days are over and you rest with your fathers, I will raise up your offspring to succeed you, who will come from your own body, and I will establish his kingdom. *He is the one who will build a house for my Name, and I will establish the throne of his kingdom forever… Your house and your kingdom will endure forever before me; your throne will be established for ever.'"*

Here in the above passage, we see how God shows His generosity beyond all bounds when he reciprocates David with his promise that He will establish David's throne forever. What did David do to deserve such a mighty endowment of a kingdom and throne that will last forever and ever? Not much. He just expressed his burning desire and a yearning to build a house for the ark of God to be housed in. But God's heart melted out of compassion and was moved by pity and the deepest love possible for David. **This is for David expressing just a passing compassion for the condition of the ark of God that was residing in a tent! What generosity on the part of God to reciprocate the tender feelings of David toward God and the ark of God! But that is typically how He feels for His children who love Him and have awe for Him and His Name!**

The second example is from the New Testament. For this we go to the Gospel of John 21:1–10 where we read:

Afterward Jesus appeared again to his disciples, by the Sea of Tiberias. It happened this way: Simon Peter, Thomas (called Didymus), Nathanael from Cana in Galilee, the sons of Zebedee, and two other disciples were together. "I'm going out to fish," Simon Peter told them, and they said, "We'll go with you." So, they went out and got into the boat, but that night they caught nothing.

Early in the morning, Jesus stood on the shore, but the disciples did not realize that it was Jesus. He called out to them, "Friends, haven't you any fish?" "No," they answered.

He said, "Throw your net on the right side *of the boat and you will find some." When they did, they were unable to haul the net in because of the large number of fish.*

Then the disciple whom Jesus loved said to Peter, "It is the Lord!" As soon as Simon Peter heard him say, "It is the Lord," he wrapped his outer garment around him (for he had taken it off) and jumped into the water. The other disciples followed in the boat, towing the net full of fish, for they were not far from shore, about a hundred yards." When they landed, they saw a fire of burning coals there with fish on it, and some bread.

Jesus said to them, "Bring some of the fish you have just caught."

Here I would like to draw your attention to the verse just above: **Jesus said to them, "Bring some of the fish you have just caught."** Were they the ones who could rightfully take credit for catching the fish which they just hauled in into the shore? Absolutely not! But Jesus gave them credit for all that fish which they caught even though the catch was made possible only because they threw the net on the right side of the boat at the call of Jesus's command to do so!

Well, once again, this is a typical example of Jesus's generosity beyond any stretch of imagination of which examples are so many in the Bible. That is how generous and compassionate our Jesus is!

In conclusion, the only reason God revealed to me the four-step formula for being born again, which has been hidden for all these years and centuries, is His infinite compassion and generosity toward me and the whole mankind that is perishing. May all the glory be to Jesus, our Savior, King, Lord, and everything! Praise the Lord, hallelujah!

Reason 8

I have more reasons to believe that this book will promote God's glory more than David did by slaying the Giant Goliath!

As I am writing this book, I do recognize that I have almost no chance of accomplishing what I am attempting to do here when I look around and see how crazy the world around me is right now and how miserably the church leaders have failed in the recent and remote past to conquer the influence of Satan, who has been having a field day ravaging them and leading astray the church of Jesus Christ in the recent past few centuries! But I am encouraged by the fact that there are many ways in which the Lord has been preparing me for this assignment. I thank the Lord Jesus Christ for the many favors that He has showered on me during the past twenty-five years for which I have only His grace to thank.

I believe that I have more and greater advantages going in my favor than David had when he went out against Goliath, as you can see from my life both in the recent past as well as in my not-so-recent past life. The years ranging over the past twenty-five years, during which time my life has been an experiment to prove to myself that what I read twenty-five years ago is 100 percent trustworthy, is of tremendous value and enrichment to my entire life both during the past twenty-five years that went by as well as to the life that I am about to enter into for glorifying the Lord by doing what I will do according to the prompting of the Spirit, who has taken control of my life especially after I have become a born-again Christian.

First, David had the five smooth stones that he used against Goliath, which he selected from the ravine nearby as we read in 1 Samuel 17:40. In my case, the Lord Jesus, in whom I have put my trust in, has shown me the four-step formula by which I was able to become a born-again Christian and thus had much more than the five smooth stones that David was able to fill the pouch of his shepherd's bag. In John 7:37, we read about Jesus saying, "If anyone is thirsty, let him come to me and drink. Whoever believes in me, as the Scripture has said, streams of living water will flow from within him."

From these rivers, I had so many types of stones of many categories to aim at Satan to destroy his tactics and schemes. I have acquired so many pieces of armor that I picked up from the many books of the Word of God such as the books of Proverbs, Ecclesiastes, and the fourteen letters of Paul, each of them with many chapters such as the letter to the Corinthians, Galatians, Ephesians, Philippians, and Colossians—two letters to the Thessalonians, two letters to Timothy, two letters of Peter, three letters of John, one letter to Hebrews with thirteen chapters in it, etc. to protect me from the attacks of Satan.

I have been given so much spiritual food that has nourished my soul and body with a balanced diet from the Gospels of Mathew, Mark, Luke, and John for my spiritual health and upkeep, etc. I can go on and on. But it is an undeniable truth that the wisdom from the Word of God has built me up in a wholesome manner so much so that I have become a believer in what Jesus told the Pharisees in John 10:34–35. Here we read Jesus telling them that "to whomever did the Word of God come, they would become like God Himself," which had the greatest impact on my entire life more than anything else.

David was able to overcome Goliath because he was Spirit-filled. This was the reason why he was able to live the way he did, achieving many accomplishments such as defeating Goliath, tearing up bears and lions, etc. But more remarkable was that he burned with love for God which prompted him to write hymns and songs and psalms, play musical instruments to praise and worship God, and lead many on the path of righteousness as he refers to in Psalm 51. But David was not Spirit-controlled, which was the reason why he was not able to avoid adultery with Bathsheba and the sin of murdering her husband to cover up his sin of adultery, etc.

But without sounding arrogant, the fact that I have been born again has given me the added advantage over David—the advantage of being Spirit-controlled. When one is born again, it is possible to avoid sin altogether even though it takes a lot of self-discipline and effort to grow in godliness and holiness and many other virtues and also to grow in the fruits and gifts of the Holy Spirit. Thus, it was the fact that I was a born-again Christian that enabled me to lead a life without *willfully sinning* after I became a born-again Christian. As I have illustrated under the topic of how one can be born again using the four steps that I have explained in this book, one can manage to live without committing any *willful sins* with a certain level of additional effort to stay away from sin. This is what 1 John 3:9 also teaches, which again I have explained under the topic of becoming a born-again Christian.

The only reason why I could avoid willful sin in my life, which eliminated my need to go for periodic confession as Catholics normally do, is the fact that I have been a born-again Christian during the years that followed after I became one. As I stated above, this is supported by John 3:9 and 1 John 5:18. Once again, I am confident that this will give me the ability to bring many others also to such an *elevated level of spirituality* which will enable them also to live without willful sins in their lives. I sincerely believe that this is an advantage that is available to us Christians, both Catholics and non-Catholics alike, which was not available to people who lived in the Old Testament times. This is the reason why Jesus said about John the Baptist in Luke 7:28, "I tell you, among those born of women there is no one greater than John; yet the one who is least in the kingdom of God is greater than he."

This was also a fact that gave me a great incentive to write this book because, after all, the purpose for which God chose us to be created was "to be holy and blameless in his sight." And this becomes a reality in our lives when we become born-again Christians by living "a holy and blameless" life (Eph. 1:4) in his sight as we read in 1 John 3:9 and 1 John 5:18 and Psalm 19:13, which

I have explained in detail under the benefits of being perfected as a born-again Christian after one has become one.

In one way, I would say that this is the most important reason why I am writing this book because it is only when we are able to live without willful sin that God's purpose and dream for creating mankind is being realized, which I am sure is the most precious trait in us that is most pleasing to God!

However, there is another reason also which is equally important, which is to glorify God in an altogether new way. For this we go to 1 Samuel 17:47 where David says, "All those gathered here will know that it is not by sword or spear that the LORD saves; for the battle is the LORD'S, and he will give all of you into our hands." This surely was a remarkable thing that David was able to achieve as a Spirit-filled warrior for God, which he prophesied before he won the victory over Goliath. This victory announced to the entire world that the power behind the victory that David won was that of God, which must have persuaded many to turn to the God of Israel and believe in Him as well as to live for Him! It was the Holy Spirit who worked through David to give him victory over the Philistines by slaying Goliath, their leader.

In my case, as I am a born-again Christian. I am not only beyond being Spirit-filled, but also Spirit-controlled, which will be true when a disciple of Christ is born again and then perfected in godliness and holiness as I have explained in my four steps to becoming a born-again Christian. With the added advantage of being Spirit-controlled over and beyond being Spirit-filled, by the abundance of grace showered on me through the process of being Spirit-controlled and then being perfected as a Spirit controlled Christian, I have almost unlimited power of the Spirit at my disposal. By using this tremendous divine power, I am now confident that one of the promises God made to me years ago while I was attending a church service in Houston will come to pass, which I never thought could be achieved.

During this vision, the LORD spoke to me through Ezekiel 17:22–24, which reads as follows:

This is what the SOVEREIGN LORD says:

"I myself will take a shoot from the very top of a cedar and plant it; I will break off a tender sprout from its topmost shoots and plant it on a high and lofty mountain. On the mountain heights of Israel, I will plant it; it will produce branches and bear fruit and become a splendid cedar. Birds of every kind will nest in it; they will find shelter in the shade of its branches. All the trees of the field will know that the LORD bring down the tall tree and make the low tree grow tall. I dry up the green tree and make the dry tree flourish."
I the LORD have spoken, and I will do it.

I am interpreting this message as the Lord telling me that by the grace of God and as a Spirit-filled and Spirit-controlled Christian, the Lord will empower me to spread the gospel and especially the message of the need for everyone to be born again in accordance with what Jesus told Nicodemus in John 3:5. Here Jesus says, "I tell you the truth, no one can enter the kingdom of God unless he is born of water and the Spirit." At the time, the Lord spoke to me and gave me this promise. I was neither a born-again Christian nor did I know what *being born again* even meant. Now when I look back and see how this message was given to me and how Jesus has been pruning me to get ready for the fulfillment of this promise in my case, I am 100 percent convinced that this is going to happen. This gives me tremendous joy which is unparalleled in any way by the enormity of this achievement.

The Holy Spirit is interpreting to me that the fulfillment of this promise will mean that a very huge number of believers, probably in the neighborhood of fifteen million, will become born-again Christians as a result of this book and that the Lord will make sure that all these millions of souls I will be able to see when I go to heaven. Such a promise has given me the greatest joy in my entire life. After all, Jesus tells us in John 15:16, "You did not choose me, but I chose you and appointed you to go and bear fruit—fruit that will last. Then the Father will give you whatever you ask in my name."

At this time, I am experiencing an overwhelming joy knowing that by producing this book as a result of all the hard work behind it, I am giving credit only to the Lord for opening my inner eyes to grasp the greatness of undertaking this project. Once again, it was only His grace that inspired me to put in all that effort during the past twenty-five years to study the Word of God and thus to be filled with the Word of God, which has made this book and the many dreams surrounding this book a reality. My heart is overflowing with joy for the mighty grace that the Lord has showered on me to make this happen.

The achievement of producing this book is like the emergence of a beautiful butterfly after going through the stages of being a worm first and then a cocoon and then finally a butterfly. Here I am comparing the hard work and the sacrifices that went before the emergence of this book to the worm and the cocoon. But as we read in Psalm 73:23–24, "…You hold me by my right hand. You guide me with your counsel." I feel that the Lord was holding my hand all these years and especially through these past twenty-five years! I'm praising the Lord for the mighty favor that He has showered on me all these years even though I have often slacked off in pursuing His counseling to me to "be diligent in Spirit to serve the Lord" (Rom. 12:11).

Reason 9

Wait a minute! Who sold you this *Another Gospel?* which is no gospel at all (when the focus on Christ is lost)?

In 2 Corinthians 11:3, we read about the anxiety that Paul experienced over the way the Corinthians were being led astray into a gospel different from the one that he and the other apostles were preaching. The gospel that they were preaching was focused on leading them to "a sincere and pure devotion to Christ." He was noticing that they were turning to a different Jesus other than the Jesus that Paul preached and to a different spirit than the one they received from Paul. Paul was afraid that this *another gospel* that they were being led into was a different gospel than the one he and the other apostles were preaching and the one accepted by Paul. In other words, Paul wanted to clarify that there are two different versions of the Gospel: the Pauline version and an *easy version*, which I refer to here as an *easier version*, which is currently being propagated by the Catholic church.

According to Paul and as we read in Isaiah 28:16, the only true version of the theology on salvation is his version. The *easier version*, which currently is in existence in some Christian faiths (including the Catholic Church), has some crucial differences from Paul's version of the Gospel. My purpose in writing this book is to alert Christians and especially those Christians who may be believing that devotion to Mary and certain saints may guarantee their salvation by substituting their Marian devotion and devotion to saints to offset for the weakness in their Christian faith.

Here I am only alerting against such false belief that some Catholics and other believers of similar faith sharing their faith in this regard may be in danger of losing their salvation. These believers may be under the impression that if their faith is weak, they can use devotion to saints as a crutch to bypass the requirement of a strong faith to be saved and thus go to heaven. Such believers cling on to devotions to Mary or Michael the Archangel or St. Jude who is often called the patron saint who can obtain for us even *impossible blessings* from God, which would otherwise be not possible. All these false notions about salvation are deceptive and extremely dangerous. The only faith that can earn eternal salvation for us is a strong faith in Jesus Christ and Jesus Christ *only* as I have pointed out through many verses and clarifications on this subject from Isaiah, Paul, and Peter in this chapter on the dangers of being misled into a *different Gospel.*

As we are reaching the end of the church age, I am inclined to strongly believe that it is a matter of life and death to clarify beyond any doubt about the need to trust in Christ and Christ alone for our eternal salvation. Our eternal salvation is so precious that just as we are alerted by Isaiah in Isaiah 28:16, it is far better to be safe than sorry. Making a wrong decision in this matter is a risk too great to take, and that is the point Paul is trying to make in the various parts of his Pauline version of the interpretation of the Gospel such as in Philippians 3:8–10. Here he writes, "I consider everything a loss compared to the surpassing greatness of knowing Christ Jesus my Lord, for whose sake I have lost all things. I consider them rubbish, that I may gain Christ and be found in him, not having a righteousness of my own that comes from the law, but that which is through faith in Christ—the righteousness that comes from God and is by faith."

Peter and Jude also express their strong concerns about relying on this *easier version* of the theology of salvation. For example, in 1 Peter 4:18, Peter writes, "If it is hard for the righteous to be saved, what will become of the ungodly and the sinner?" And Paul says in Romans 3:10, "There is no one righteous, not even one; there is no one who understands, no one who seeks God."

With that said, first of all, let us see what Isaiah says in the Old Testament before we get to the Pauline version of what I will call the *sure foundation* on which the Pauline version of the teaching on the theology of salvation is built. By this what I mean is that the Pauline version of the New Testament interpretation of the theology on salvation is much safer than the *easier version* of the same even though the *easier version* is a *good start* for new believers whom I call *beginners* here.

There are three reasons why the *easier version* of the interpretation of the theology on salvation is either too risky or inadequate to earn salvation for anyone. I would like to elaborate on each of these three reasons below from the various standpoints taken both from the Old Testament as well as New Testament.

First reason:

In Isaiah 28:16–17, we read, "This is what the sovereign Lord says, 'See, I lay a stone in Zion, a tested stone, a precious cornerstone for a sure foundation; the one who trusts will never be dismayed. I will make justice the measuring line and righteousness the plumb line; hail will sweep away your refuge, the lie, and water will overflow your hiding place."

In this passage, by saying "water will overflow your hiding place," God is saying that anyone who relies on anyone else or anything else will be destroyed because it is nothing but a lie. Paul also talks about the exclusivity of trusting in God and no one else when he writes about his testimony about God in 1 Corinthians 2:2 where he says, "For I resolved to know nothing while I was with you except Jesus Christ and him crucified." Again in 1 Peter 2:6–8, Peter also talks about the exclusivity of Jesus Christ as the only source of salvation. Here he writes:

> For in Scripture it says: "See, I lay a stone in Zion, a chosen and precious cornerstone, and the one who trusts in him, will never be put to shame."
>
> "Now to you who believe, this stone is precious. But to those who do not believe,

"The stone the builders rejected has become
the capstone,"
And, "A stone that causes men to stumble and
a rock that makes them fall." They stumble because they disobey the message.

Again in John 14:6, Jesus says, "No one comes to the Father except through me."

Once again, Jesus Himself emphasizes the exclusivity of Himself as the one and only source of our salvation. As though these were not enough, in Hebrews 12:2, we are asked to "fix our eyes on Jesus, the author and perfecter of our faith, who for the joy set before him endured the cross." Once again, we are given another example in the case of Lot's wife in Genesis 19:17 where we are told that Lot's wife was turned into a pillar of salt for looking back, which was the least of the four commands that Lot and his wife were given as they were fleeing Sodom and Gomorrah even as she was holding on to the arm of the angel just as her husband also was. But he did not look back holding on to the hand of the angel and thus was saved. Thus, we see here as well as from Jesus's own saying to us that "one who places his hand on the plough and looks back is not worthy of me," it is very clear that we have to be single-focused when we are following Christ in our spiritual life. We cannot afford to take even the slightest risk of disobeying even one of the smallest commands (such as one regarding a single look back) that Jesus gives us as we are pilgrimaging toward our eternal home in heaven.

I have to warn you of one more thing, which is the fact that as we continue in our spiritual journey, we cannot even trust our own heart as we read in Jeremiah 17:9, "The heart is deceitful above all things and beyond cure." And this is the reason why Jesus tells us in John 3:5 that we "must be born again" if we want to enter the kingdom of heaven because the only way to get a brand-new heart is to become a born-again Christian! This is also the reason why I have chosen the subject of being born again as the central theme of this book.

Second reason:

The second reason why the *easier version* of the theology on salvation is inadequate to take us to heaven is that God cannot lead us on the path of salvation if we are not mature Christians by being trained in the Word of God as we read in Isaiah 28:9. Here we read, "Who is it he is trying to teach? To whom is he explaining his message? To children weaned from the milk to those just taken from the breast?" This is a rhetorical question to which the answer is also given by the Prophet Isaiah. We can be trained by God ONLY if our faith has matured over the years by submitting ourselves to the Word of God and digesting it through a deeper understanding of what it means and putting into practice what the Word of God is asking us to do. And that too, it has to be put into practice day in and day out until it becomes a way of life for a child of God who wants to grow in the Word of God.

A related passage is found in the New Testament in Hebrews 5:11–14 where we read,

> We have much to say about this, but it is hard to explain because you are slow to learn. In fact, though by this time you ought to be teachers, you need someone to teach you the elementary truths of God's Word all over again. You need milk, not solid food! Anyone who lives on milk, being still an infant, is not acquainted with the teaching about righteousness. But solid food is for the mature, who by constant use have trained themselves to distinguish good from evil.

As a remedy to change this situation, St. Paul is asking those who are immature and are still in the beginning stage of their studies on Christ by advancing to the next level and to the level after that and so on at the beginning of chapter 6. Thus, in Hebrews 6:1–2, we read,

> Therefore, let us leave the elementary teachings about Christ and go on to maturity, not lay-

ing again the foundation of repentance from acts that lead to death, and of faith in God, instruction about baptisms, the laying on of hands, the resurrection of the dead, and eternal judgment.

Third reason:

There is a third reason why the *easier version* of the theology on salvation encourages believers to hold on to devotion to Mary, the mother of Jesus, and devotion to certain saints is that it gives a false hope that these devotions will keep them from the fires of eternal hell. For example, those who pray the Hail Mary prayer are inclined to believe that the portion "Pray for us, sinners, now and at the hour of our death" in this prayer is powerful enough to save them so as to avoid going to hell. But this is not true because such a false assurance and complacency are based on the assumption that God's righteousness and way of thinking are the same as man's righteousness and way of thinking. As a result, many Catholics believe that if they repeatedly pray for Mary's intercession at the time of their death, Mary will intercede for them in front of Jesus when all of us including those believers who rely on Mary's intercession appear in front of the judgment seat of Jesus as we read in 2 Corinthians 5:10.

Let us examine some of the scriptural passages which disprove this false notion. For example, in the Old Testament in Isaiah 28:16–17, we read,

> This is what the sovereign Lord says:
> "See, I lay a stone in Zion, a tested stone, a precious cornerstone for a sure foundation; the one who trusts will never be dismayed.
> I will make justice the measuring line and righteousness he plumbline; hail will sweep away your refuge, the lie, and water will overflow your hiding place."

Notice that as we saw above in our first reason why the *easier version* of the theology on salvation will not work when it comes to assuring our salvation, the only cornerstone that we have to go by is Christ and Christ alone. We saw that if we don't conform to the cornerstone who is Christ, then Christ the Cornerstone will become Christ the stumbling stone for all those who use the intercession of Mary and/or St. Jude as we read in 1 Peter 2:8. There is no exception to this truth mentioned anywhere in the Word of God that contradicts this truth!

Within the context of Mary, the mother of Jesus, interceding for those Catholics who most assuredly believe that Mary will intercede for them, many of them quote Mary interceding on behalf of the bridegroom at the wedding banquet in Cana when the wine ran out. But if we carefully read the narration of the event when Jesus turned water into wine during the banquet in Cana, we can see that the only thing Mary said to the servants was, "Do whatever he tells you." Thus, we can see that Mary did not do anything that can be interpreted as interceding on behalf of the bridegroom to save his reputation which was at stake here. What Mary said was only to obey the Word of God spoken by Jesus during that banquet. Mary would say the same thing if we were to confront the same challenge today also instead of carrying out any intercession for us, which she did not do at that banquet at Cana either.

In this case, I would like to point out one verse from 2 Corinthians 5:16. Here we read, "So from now on, we regard no one from a worldly point of view. Though we once regarded Christ in this way, we do so no longer." If we stay within the meaning of this verse and think of Jesus as someone who is outside the realm of someone who would treat his mother as a son would normally do, we would be right in thinking that Jesus would listen to the intercession of Mary since she was His mother once upon a time when Jesus and Mary were son and mother on this earth. But that is no longer the case and therefore, the normal human way of responding to a mother's request is no longer applicable to Jesus and Mary anymore. That is what the above verse 2 Corinthians 5:16 here implies.

Once again, there are many who think that we need somebody like Mary or some saints to intercede for us because we are big sinners, and therefore, if we ask Jesus directly for the remission of our sins, He may not listen to us. This is also a misconception, which we will be convinced of when we read about the two criminals who hung on the cross on either side of the cross of Jesus. In Luke 23:39–43, we read about these criminals. While one of the two was hurling insults at Jesus, the other one turned first to his counterpart who was insulting Jesus and said to him, "Don't you fear God," he said, "since you are under the same sentence? We are punished justly, for we are getting what our deeds deserve. But this man has done nothing wrong." Then he said, "Jesus, remember me when you come into your kingdom." Jesus answered him, "I tell you the truth. Today you will be with me in paradise."

Here the criminal who cried out to Jesus could have asked Mary, the mother of Jesus, who was standing at the foot of the cross, to intercede for him. But he did not do that. And I don't think most of us are greater sinners than this criminal; at least most of us have not been found guilty by any court of deserving of the death penalty! This criminal also teaches that if we repent of our sins and cry out to Jesus, we will be forgiven by Jesus just as he was forgiven. Let not anyone tell you otherwise. After all, we have to remember what we read in Hebrews 10:14, "By one sacrifice he [Jesus] has made perfect forever those who are being made holy."

Then why are we so scared to approach Jesus to ask for His forgiveness? And we don't even have to call on Jesus for forgiveness if we follow the four steps to become a born-again Christian, which is the theme of this book. Because if we are born again and hold on to the sanctity that we got when we were born again by pursuing the steps to remain and grow in the perfection that we got when we were born again, as we read in 1 John 3:9 and 1 John 5:18, we can say goodbye to sin once and for all, and we won't ever have to go for confession in our life! After all, living without sin was the purpose why God created us for as we read in Ephesians 1:4. Here we read, "He chose us in him before the creation of the world to be holy and blameless in his sight."

Here, also the reason why we tend to go through Mary to seek forgiveness for our sins or for that matter to receive any favor from Jesus is that once again, we forget the principle that the Word of God lays in front of us in 2 Corinthians 5:16. We think of the relationship between Jesus and Mary in human terms, which is the wrong thing to do since it is not consistent with what this verse tells us. In fact, the right principle that we should adopt in this case is the one contained in Psalm 103:2–4, which says,

> Praise the Lord, O my soul, and forget not all
> his benefits—
> who forgives all your sins and heals all your
> diseases,
> who redeems your life from the pit and crowns
> you with love and compassion.

So believe me when I say, "You can do it." Because God says so here! And I am a living witness to the truth that we can most assuredly believe Him because I have, as a result of my personal experience in my spiritual life, found out something that is much bigger than even this: ***We can live as another Christ in this sinful world if we become born again Christians by following the four-step process to do it explained in this book and make a commitment to be filled with the Word of God.*** I am saying this based on the results of my personal experiment with the Word of God, specifically speaking, with what we read in John 10:34–35.

Yes, my personal life that started on October 27, 1979, was nothing but a faith journey that proved to me the truthfulness of the promise Jesus gives us in John 10:34–35 that if we become filled with the Word of God, we can also become like another Christ and live like another Christ in this dark world as I have discovered and explained in this book for you also to discover and live out. And being born again is the centerpiece of such an abundant Christian living that Jesus promised us in John 10:10, which is made possible by following the four-step process for becoming a born-again Christian and by being filled with the Word of God, day in and day out, each minute and second of our life! If I can do it, you can do it also. The reason I say this is that when I was a teenager, I was not only a low self-esteemed boy but also had an awkward personality with a tendency to freeze up in social settings especially if I had to speak even a single word in front of the public! But now I can speak in front of the public for hours if needed especially if it is about the Word of God!

Conclusion

There is a big difference between the way Peter approached the person of Mary and the way Paul viewed Mary, the mother of Jesus. The reason for this difference is explained by Paul in 2 Corinthians 5:16 where he writes: "So, from now on we regard no one from a worldly point of view. Though we once regarded Christ in this way, we do so no longer." From what the Holy Spirit has shown me, the reason why Paul was able to grow into a spiritual maturity, which was not attained by Peter or any other apostle, is the fact that he viewed Jesus in an almost entirely different way than Peter saw Jesus. As we read above in 2 Corinthians 5:16, Peter viewed Mary, the mother of Jesus, from a more worldly point of view than Paul. As a result, Paul was able to grow spiritually more mature than Peter. This was one of the reasons why Paul had a greater focus on Jesus than Peter, whose perception of Mary as the mother of Jesus permeated throughout the Catholic Church through centuries even up to this day. This explains why the Catholic Church gives so much importance to the devotion to Mary than Paul as evident from the many traditions of the Catholic Church. This must have been the reason that Paul wrote in 1 Corinthians 2:2: "For I resolved to know nothing while I was with you except Jesus Christ and him crucified."

I am increasingly more convinced as days go by that as we read also in Hebrews 12:1–2, the right perspective that we should have in our spiritual life as we run our race with perseverance is that we should fix our eyes on Jesus, the author and finisher of our faith, and should not be distracted from our fixation on Christ in any way whatsoever, not even by Mary, who we know is truly the mother of Jesus and respect her for that. In this respect and all other respects, we have to go by the Word of God, which repeatedly tells us that Christ is our first love, and we should never compromise on this truth as the Holy

Spirit tells us in Revelation 2:4. Not forsaking our first love, who is Jesus and no one else, should not be compromised in which case our eyes are no longer fixed on *the author and finisher of our faith.*

In 1 Peter 2:6, God tells us that He lays "a stone in Zion, a chosen and precious cornerstone and the one who trusts in him will never be put to shame." When God gives us such an ironclad assurance, we better believe it and should not be distracted by anyone else or anything else contrary to what God says and, thus, be deceived. Our fixation on Christ should never be compromised. If we do, be on guard as to what verse 1 Peter 2:7–8 says:

> "The stone the builders rejected has become
> the capstone,"
> And, "
> A stone that causes men to stumble and a rock
> that makes them fall."
> They stumble because they disobey the message— which is also what they were destined for.

The above two verses simply mean that if we stumble on Christ, who alone is our cornerstone (a stone to which we all should make every effort to be aligned), we are certainly going to "stumble" and Christ, who alone is the only cornerstone there is, will become for us a rock that will make us fall.

This very important truth is also ascertained and explained by Isaiah in Isaiah 28:16–17 where we read:

> See, I lay a stone in Zion, a tested stone, a precious cornerstone for a sure foundation;
> The one who trusts will never be dismayed.
> I will make justice the measuring line and righteousness the plumb line;
> Hail will sweep away your refuge, the lie, and water will overflow your hiding place.

Here Isaiah is confirming what Peter writes in 1 Peter 6:7 and further adds to it. Isaiah says that Jesus Christ alone is going to be the sure foundation as God is going to justice the measuring line and righteousness the plumb line, which means God will ensure in the final judgment that justice and righteousness are going to be the ultimate foundation on which His kingdom is going to be founded on. This even strikes a clear warning for those who rely on crutches like devotion to Mary or other saints for their eternal salvation. Because as we read in Ephesians 2:8: "It is by grace we have been saved, through faith—and this is not from yourselves, it is the gift of God—not by works, so that no one can boast." If we try to substitute God's terms for our salvation, it is not going to work because to receive God's salvation, we have to pursue it according to the terms laid out by God, which says that He (Christ) alone is our *sure foundation* (Isaiah 28:16). Isaiah goes on to say that anything else to be used as a refuge is "a lie and water overflow on those who hide under such a lie" (Isaiah 28:17). Thus, Isaiah makes it very clear that no one can go beyond Jesus Christ who alone is our only means by which we can go to heaven just as this truth is also confirmed by Acts 4:12. Here it says: "Salvation is found in no one else, for there is no other name under heaven given to men by which we can be saved." In this context, what Paul writes in 1 Corinthians 13:11 is so relevant. Here he tells us: "When I was a child, I talked like a child, I thought like a child, I reasoned like a child. When I became a man, I put childish ways behind me. Now we see but a poor reflection as in a mirror; then we shall see face to face. Now I know in part, then I shall know fully, even as I am fully known." In my Spirit-inspired opinion, using our limited knowledge, it is foolishness to change the terms of God, which He has laid down to be satisfied for our eternal salvation. It is a risk too great to ill afford as we are warned in Proverbs 14:12: "There is a way that seems right to a man, but in the end, it leads to death."

In my humble opinion, to grow from the level of the Christian maturity of Peter to that of Paul, we certainly need to keep our focus strictly on Christ and Christ alone. I do know that this will upset a lot of my fellow Catholics. But I am writing this not merely for Catholics but for anyone who wants to be a disciple of Christ like Paul. As

Paul writes in Philippians 4:8–9: "Finally, brothers, whatever is true, whatever is noble, whatever is right, whatever is true, whatever is noble, whatever is right, whatever is pure, whatever is lovely, whatever is admirable—if anything is excellent or praiseworthy— think about such things. Whatever you have learned or received or heard from me or seen in me—put it into practice. And the God of peace will be with you." What I am wishing for you here is that you always have perfect peace and that you always have God also with you because perfect peace can come only from God!

When we are born again, as we read in John 16:9, Holy Spirit will convict us "in regard to sin, because men do not believe in Jesus." There is a reason why Jesus says this because man is saved by grace through faith according to Ephesians 2:8. Unless we are born again, we cannot receive the Holy Spirit, and unless we have the Holy Spirit, we cannot be convicted of the greatest sin, which is lack of faith. On the other hand, if we have the Holy Spirit, he will convict us of our lack of faith as we read in John 16:9. This is also the reason that Paul tells us in Romans 8:9 that "anyone who does not have the Spirit of Christ does not belong to Christ." Thus, the devotion to Mary is one of the greatest deceptions that Satan uses to keep us away from being born again. Because, as we read in Hebrews 4:16, we can boldly approach the throne of grace so that we "may obtain mercy and find grace to help us in our time of every need" since we have Jesus as our high priest who has been tempted in every way, just as we are." Let not anyone tell you otherwise in this regard. If anyone does, boldly we should tell that someone, "Get behind me, Satan" because he/she is deceiving you by sowing seeds of doubt in your minds and souls.

What Satan does in the case of those who go to Mary or other saints for intercession is that he gives a sense of inadequacy or inferiority to make them feel unworthy to go straight to Christ for the remission of their sins. Thus, he makes them think that going to Mary will be the best solution to overcome their lack of faith in Jesus, which is as good as going to Jesus. This is a great deception because of the reasons I explained above as Jesus alone is the sure foundation on which our salvation depends. A Christian who depends on Mary or any other saints like St. Jude or St. Michael is being deceived by

Satan and is falling into the trap of Satan. But when a Christian is born again, he receives the Holy Spirit who convicts him of the need to go to Christ who alone is the only one in whose name one can be saved as we read in Acts 4:12. This is the reason why I have become a strong advocate to tell Christians that if they want to go to heaven, they must be born again as Jesus said to Nicodemus in John 3:3.

As the final word on this, I like to point out that not even Peter, the first Pope, understood Paul as Paul went around everywhere during the early period of the church, preaching about the absolute need to be born again to go to heaven. For Paul, this was the most important step in being saved. Therefore, he preached this absolutely needed step of salvation most passionately wherever he went as we read in Acts 19:2. Not only he preached about being born again, but he stressed the importance of living as Christ in his personal life as an apostle and as a great imitator of Christ, which he recommended his followers also to imitate him in the best way possible. Thus, in Acts 26:29, Paul says to King Agrippa: "Short time or long—I pray God that not only you but all who are listening to me today may become what I am, except for these chains." For him to say this to others was not easy. For example, regarding his own personal life, he says in 1 Corinthians 9:27: "I do not run like a man running aimlessly. I do not fight like a man beating the air. No, I beat my body and make it my slave so that after I have preached to others, I myself will not be disqualified for the prize." No wonder he was able to say in Philippians 1:21: "For me, to live is Christ and to die is gain."

This was also the reason why even Peter admitted that he was rather lost when it came to understanding Paul. Thus, he says in 2 Peter 3:15: "Just as our dear brother Paul also wrote you with the wisdom that God gave him… His letters contain some things that are hard to understand, which ignorant and unstable people distort as they do the other Scriptures, to their own destruction." The only reason that I believe how Paul got so much wisdom, which greatly surprised even Peter who was the first Pope of the Catholic Church, is that unlike anyone else in the entire Bible, Paul was the most ardent advocate and promoter of the need of every Christian to be born again.

Reason 10

Wait a minute! Who sold you this *Another Gospel?* which is no gospel at all (an examination of the theology on the Lord's Table)?

In the beginning of this book, when I addressed the various reasons why I wrote this book, one of the reasons I gave is to convince us of the urgent need for us who have been blessed to know the true God to become born-again Christians. One of the main reasons why this world that we are living in is so badly messed up is that we who know God have no awe for God and are not willing to mend our ways and return to God by correcting our theological errors and sinful habits. The examples are many and complex, but the solution is fairly simple although it is not hard and feasible to correct if we really want to do it. The problem we are facing and its solutions have various aspects that need to be addressed. Looking at a glance, there are mainly four aspects to the problem we are facing namely,

1. Where did we go wrong?
2. What are the consequences we are facing?
3. Why the Urgency to correct our mistakes? And
4. Why only God can help us to return to Him

Where we went wrong?

In 1 Corinthians 4:6, we read, "Do not go beyond what is written." It seems all our problems started with us not paying attention to what the Holy Spirit told us all along the pages of the written Scriptures. We chose to deviate from the written Word of God even though we had stern warnings such as in Deuteronomy 32:46–47. Here we read, "Take to heart all the words I have solemnly declared to you this day, so that you may command your children to obey carefully all the words of this law. They are not just idle words for you—they are your life. By them, you will live long in the land you are crossing the Jordan to possess." So it was clear that what was expected of the Israelites was wholehearted obedience to the Word of God and the warning was stern enough. But what did they do, and what have we done with the Word of God?

For this kind of obedience, even Jesus had shown us examples of when He was tempted in the desert after His forty days of fasting. He was tempted three times as we read in Matthew 4:3, 4:6, and 4:8. In the first temptation, He was asked to turn stones into bread to which His response was: "It is written: 'Man does not live on bread alone, but on every word that comes from the mouth of God.'" In the same way, Jesus overcame the second and third temptations also by giving replies to Satan both starting with "It is written…" However, in the case of the second temptation, His answer started with: "It is also written." By this, Jesus was demonstrating to us that we should know not only what is "written" but also what is "also written." In other words, we should have a thorough understanding of what the Word of God says in each circumstance that we face in life, the circumstances in which God has said what He has said, and also if there was anything else that God has said elsewhere regarding what God has already said!

Now let us examine what the Word of God says about the Bereans in Acts 17:11, which gives us a glimpse into the tenacity of the Bereans to make sure that they would only believe what they heard from Paul only after verifying that what Paul preached was consistent with what the Word of God said in the Scriptures. Thus, in Acts 17:11, we read, "Now the Bereans were of more noble character than the Thessalonians, for they received the message with great eagerness and examined the Scriptures every day to see if what Paul said was true." This kind of insistence on the part of the Bereans when it comes to listening and obeying the Word of God earned them the title "more noble Bereans" in the esteem of the Holy Spirit who is the real author of the text in the Acts of the Apostles as in the case in every other text in the rest of the Word of God is.

Unfortunately, what has happened in the church and especially in the largest segment of the church of Christ, which is the Roman Catholic church, is not consistent with the truth found in the Word of God. Thus, some major and embarrassing theological errors have resulted which fact has, in turn, resulted in the way the worship is being held within the Catholic church. There are mainly two errors that have happened, one affecting the worship and the other affecting the way we honor God. Let us see these two errors in detail.

How the worship has been impacted

Regarding the Holy Eucharist, which is basically the consecrated bread and the consecrated blood that the congregation members partake of during the Holy Mass, Jesus says in John 6:55, "For my flesh is real food and my blood is real drink." Accordingly, the priest says during and as part of the consecration, "This is my body" when consecrating the bread, and "This is my blood" when consecrating the wine. But within five minutes or so after, at the communion service, the priest holds the same consecrated bread in his hand and says: "Behold the Lamb of God who takes away the sins of the world; happy are they who are called to the feast of the Lamb." This is where the problem lies. The same bread which the priest held in his hand a few minutes ago is now being referred to as the lamb of God, which is the personal and endearing name of Jesus Christ, the second person of the Holy Trinity who became our sacrificial lamb to pay atonement for our sins by dying on the cross two thousand years ago.

This is so wrong to address the consecrated bread as though it is the person of Jesus Christ Himself for six reasons: first, it was called the body of Christ just a few minutes ago by the priest who just consecrated the bread; secondly, it is a contradiction of what Jesus calls it in John 6:55 calling the bread His body; and there is also a third reason why it is wrong to call the consecrated bread the Lamb of God, which means that there is the real presence of Jesus Christ in that bread. This contradicts Isaiah 57:15 wherein God says: "I live in a high and holy place, but also with him who is contrite and lowly in spirit to revive the spirit of the lowly and to revive the heart of the contrite." Thus, this is a fourth reason why it is wrong to say that there is the real presence of Jesus in the consecrated host or bread. There is a fifth reason why it is wrong to say that there is the real presence of Jesus in the consecrated bread. The fifth reason is that in Acts 17:24, we read: "The God who made the world and everything in it is the Lord of heaven and earth and does not live in temples built by hands." And finally, there is a sixth reason to believe that the consecrated bread does not have the real presence of Jesus Christ in it. If this were the case, what we read in John 13:27 would not have happened: "As soon as Judas took the bread, Satan entered into him."

When I thought about the reasons why so much confusion and darkness has entered the worship of God by the children of God, the Holy Spirit revealed to me that the reason why all this has happened is the fact that as I illustrated above at the beginning of this chapter, we have not paid enough attention to make sure that we have been adhering to the written Word of God as Jesus showed us by His own example when He was tempted three times by Satan about which we read in Matthew 4. If our ancestors had done this, they would have easily discovered that they should have done what Ephesians 6:14 required them to do but failed to do. Ephesians 6:14 commands us to make sure that we would not stumble in our faith journey as well as in our worship of God "in spirit and truth" by standing firm "with the belt of truth buckled around our waist." According to John 4:23, the only form of worship that is acceptable to the Father is the worship of God "in truth and spirit."

With that said, what is the truth that Paul is talking about in Eph. 6:14? First of all, truth is what John 17:3 says, which is, "knowing the only true God, and Jesus Christ, whom God has sent." Secondly, the truth is according to John 1:14, "The Word become flesh and made his dwelling among us. We have seen his glory, the glory of the One and Only, who came from the Father, full of grace and truth." In this case, the only true way to know the true God is to know Him in the person of Jesus Christ who is the embodiment of and the ultimate personification of grace and truth. In other words, there is no boundary or limit to both the grace and the truth that is found in Him so much so that no one can even grasp or comprehend even a splinter of the ultimate reality of the grace and truth that resides in Jesus Christ nor measure even a tiny segment of either the grace or the truth that resides in him.

If anyone even vaguely comprehended it, he or she will never even look anywhere seeking an intercessor like Mary, the mother of God or St. Jude, or anyone else. Because you cannot even absorb or comprehend even an infinitesimally tiny portion of God's grace or truth in your soul or mind because it is too much to be processed within one's mind or soul.

To borrow an example from the life history of St. Augustine, I believe it was, who while he was trying to comprehend the mystery of the Holy Trinity as he was taking a morning walk along the seashore, noticed a little boy who, with a little shell, was trying to empty the vast ocean in front of him into a fairly large hole on the beach. When St. Augustine told him, it was impossible for him to do that no matter how long or how hard he tried, the little boy told St. Augustine that it was easier for him to empty the ocean the way he was trying to do it than for St. Augustine to comprehend the mystery of the Holy Trinity. Well, let me tell you that fathoming the grace and truth that resides in Jesus Christ is harder than emptying that ocean into that puddle a million times over. I hope you get at least a vague idea of the immeasurable volume of truth and grace that reside in Jesus Christ!

Thirdly, according to John 17:17, "Thy Word is truth." The truth in the Word of God is pretty much as deep as how deep the grace and the truth which reside in the person of Jesus Christ are as I have attempted to describe above. I am sure you will give me probably an F followed by ten minuses assuming that this is the lowest grade on the evaluation scale that I can have.

Having said that, if our fathers of faith in the past had regarded the instruction for girdling their waist with the truth of God and obeyed it as we are instructed to do in Ephesians 6:14, they would not have gotten into the mess that they have gotten into with regard to the Holy Eucharist. The reason why I say this is that, if they had made a commitment to the truth, they would not have called the consecrated bread *my body* meaning the flesh of Jesus one minute and then in the next minute called it the lamb of God meaning the second person of the Holy Trinity. They would not have said that there is the real presence of Jesus in the consecrated bread that Judas received from Jesus Himself only to go and hang himself after receiving it, etc. I can go on with many other examples, but you get the gist of what I am trying to say here, I am sure!

Now at this time, since we are probably in the deepest hole possible as far as implementing the theology of we are in as far as our Christian faith is concerned with regard to the Lord's Supper, what is the remedy we have to come out of this deepest hole that we find ourselves in? Well, Jesus has the answer!

First, repent of our sins in these areas of our theology on the Lord's Supper, taking a firm resolution to correct them immediately and never to repeat them in the future. Then follow the four-step process to become born-again Christian and restart our Christian lives as precious sons and daughters of God. God is waiting for us to return to Him by taking this gigantic step by taking a huge leap of faith! If you decide to take this giant leap of faith, God who is our most loving and merciful Father is standing at the door of heaven to welcome us back with his stretched-out arms just as the father in Luke 15 who welcomed his lost son with the greatest party that you see in the entire Bible: waiting with the best robes to adorn him with, with a royal ring to put on his finger, new shoes on his feet, etc. Also, never forget that when the lost sheep is found, the good shepherd in Luke 15:5 carries it on his shoulders after searching and finding it after leaving the other ninety-nine to go in search of the lost one! He rejoices more over the lost one than the other ninety-nine which were not lost and starts a huge party and keeps it going. Now the head of the lost sheep is raised higher than even the head of the shepherd! How awesome!

Some of the unintended, though tragical, results of relegating an awesome God to the simple form of a consecrated piece of bread are:

1. Our worship is no longer one in spirit and truth. Thus, our worship is no longer the true worship that God desires from us according to what Jesus tells us in John 4:23.

2. We take God for granted because the one who receives the Lord's Supper is misled into thinking he is actually receiving Jesus Himself in His complete glory as He really is which is not the case.

3. The only way man is saved is by grace through faith. But when God's grace is misrepresented by treating a piece of consecrated bread as God Himself, God's glory is almost infinitely diminished, and thus even the very process of God's salvation plan for man is altered beyond imagination.

4. When the Lord's Supper, which is the consecrated bread and wine administered during Holy Mass, is falsely misrepresented as God Himself, then those who receive the Lord's Supper are led into thinking that the bread and wine they receive is truly God Himself in His full glory which is not true.

5. The recipients of the Lord's Supper are misled into believing in a wrong form of true spirituality. Since the consecrated bread is not true God in itself although the piece of bread is being treated as though it is, day by day, by receiving the Lord's Supper, the believer is more and more drawn into a spirituality not supported by the Word of God.

6. The false notion that we can force God to come into a piece of consecrated bread and treat God almost like a helpless puppet is an encroachment on His divinity by us who are His children and an ultimate mockery of Christian worship.

7. The false myth that God can be forced to come into our hearts regardless of our spiritual condition is an encroachment on the divine power of God and the ultimate mockery of Christian worship.

Conclusion

As you may have noticed above, there are some conflicting worship practices in the worship formats and rituals within the Catholic Church and other denominations which have some serious conflicts with theological truths as we read in the Word of God, which have to be corrected. This is because, according to Jesus in John 4:23, "a time is coming and has now come when the true worshipers will worship the Father in spirit and truth, for they are the kind of worshipers the Father seeks." Additionally, as we also read above in Psalm 145:18: "The Lord is near to all who call on him, to all who call on him in truth."

We all want God the Father to be pleased with our worship, and therefore, we want to make sure that our worship is in spirit and truth because it is the kind of worship pleasing to the Father as we saw above according to John 4:23. We also always want for God to be near to us and us to be near to God as we read above in Psalm 145. As the designated servant of God to look into the various issues that exist today in the worship practices of the various denominations today and especially within the Catholic Church, I would like to point out some serious discrepancies in the theological truths being taught and the worship practices, which have emerged based often times not in keeping with the theological truths found in the Scriptures. So in the following couple of pages, I am embarking on a journey to examine closely both the theological doctrines and the worship practices, which ought to have been compatible with each other but are often not as there are some serious heresies that exist in the worship practices, which have often caused great embarrassments among the various Christian denominations.

Particularly speaking, the main area in which these discrepancies between theology and practices exist is in the area of the Lord's Supper, which I have attempted to sort out to bring about a satisfactory alignment between theology and the corresponding practices. Admittedly, the evaluation of the compatibility between theology and worship practices may not be exhaustive, but I feel that I have made a comprehensive evaluation to make some serious corrections in the worship practices in the various denominations and especially within the Catholic Church. With that said, let me launch myself rather deeply into some of the worship practices to take a serious look at them with a view to aligning them with the "biblical truths" that Jesus laid down especially in the Gospel of John to diffuse some of these serious confusions that have occurred in the past and have established themselves over many centuries in the past.

In John 4:21–24, while speaking to the Samaritan woman, Jesus said: "Believe me, woman, a time is coming when you will worship the Father neither on this mountain nor in Jerusalem… Yet a time is coming and has now come when the true worshipers will worship the Father in spirit and truth, for they are the kind of worshipers the Father seeks. God is spirit, and his worshipers must worship in spirit and truth." Thus, it is of utmost importance that Christian worship must be carried out in spirit and truth if it is to be pleasing to God. Therefore, let me try to clear some of the misgivings and misconceptions, which have infiltrated into the worship practices of the Catholic Church in particular and in varying degrees into the worship practices of other denominations also. These misconceptions have gotten into the celebration of the Lord's Supper, which is fondly called the Eucharistic celebration within the Catholic Church.

For this, we will thoroughly evaluate our worship practices in comparison with their theological underpinnings to examine discrepancies in the way the worship practices have failed to be made compatible with the corresponding theological truths and doctrines. We are doing this to attempt to make the two compatibles with the truths in the Word of God and not vice versa, in which case such attempts would be heretical. Thus, we can and must make any necessary corrections in our worship format to ensure that our worship is carried out in spirit and truth as the Word of God dictates.

What I would like to take up as the first consideration is the most important element, probably the centerpiece of our Christian worship, which is the partaking of the bread that we do during the celebration of the Lord's Supper. Here the long-debated question is whether the bread consecrated during the worship service has the true presence of Christ in it or not. For this, let us take the verse from the Bible John 6:63 in which Jesus says: "The Spirit gives life, the flesh counts for nothing." Here the language is simple enough to easily understand what Jesus is telling us. At the same time, there is a lot of confusion among believers as to whether there is the real presence of Jesus in the consecrated bread consumed by the worshipers during the worship at the Lord's Supper.

According to Jesus, the bread does not have the real presence of himself in it as he himself says that the bread transformed into his flesh does not count for anything except as "food" for the body. I am saying this because, in John 6:55, he says: "My flesh is real food and my blood real drink." This becomes much clearer if we see what happened during the Passover that occurred in Egypt as the Israelites were escaping from their slavery under Pharaoh, the powerful arm of God as described in Exodus 12:1–50. It is to be noted here that the way in which the Israelites ate the meat of the slaughtered lamb was the forerunner of the Passover in the New Testament to come, during which the meat was eaten only as a celebration meal. However, what saved them from the slayer who passed by during that night was the blood of the lamb sprinkled on the doorframe of the houses of the Israelites. This was what Jesus meant when he said in John 6:63b that "the flesh does not count for anything" other than for food for the body of the one who partakes of it. However, since this is the flesh of the Passover lamb that was slaughtered, who in the New Testament is Christ himself, it was to be eaten with reverence and observing the many instructions reminiscent of the instructions that were given to the Israelites for eating the Passover meal as they were trying to get out of the slavery of the Pharaoh on that day described in Exodus 12.

Thus, if we remember the forerunner meal that the Israelites ate during the Passover meal described in chapter 12 of Exodus, we will get the meaning of what Jesus said in John 6:63 that "the flesh counts for nothing." It was not the meat of the lamb that they slaughtered that night that saved them from the slavery of Pharaoh, but its blood that they sprinkled on the doorframe of their houses, which the slayer who passed by their houses noticed and, thus, recognized that it was the house of an Israelite and then passed by as he was to slay only the firstborns of only those houses that belonged to the Egyptians! However, since the consecrated bread is transformed into the flesh of Jesus who is the "Passover Lamb" in the New Testament, it has to be eaten with great reverence and a pure heart and soul, free of sin as Paul warns us in 1 Corinthians 11:27–30. If we don't do it with the due reverence, which it deserves, Paul goes on to say that if anyone eats and drinks without recognizing the body of the Lord (in the Eucharist) in the celebration of the New Testament Passover meal, he eats and drinks judgment on himself. Paul also adds that "many among you are weak and sick, and a number of you have fallen asleep." Now we know that Judas fell asleep spiritually speaking (meaning that he died spiritually) when he took the bread from Jesus's own hands and ate it. That is why he betrayed Jesus so remorselessly because Satan had entered him the moment he took and ate the bread from Jesus's hands as we read in John 13:27.

But the fact remains that in the New Testament, it is not the flesh nor the blood that saves us from our sins. In that respect, our "Passover meal," during which we consume the symbolic consecrated bread and the symbolic consecrated wine, is not what serves as a ransom for our salvation as they are only symbols of the actual flesh and blood of Jesus who is our "Passover Lamb," which was sacrificed on the cross on Calvary as the real ransom for our salvation. ***This blood by which we are being saved was shed by Jesus on the cross as an expiation for our sins, which is identical to the blood sprinkled on the doorframes of the houses of the Israelites that spared the firstborns in the houses of the Israelites. That is why we read in Hebrews 10:14b: "By one sacrifice he has made perfect forever those who are being made holy."*** The symbolic bread and blood that we partake of during the Eucharistic celebration of the Mass are in memory of the Passover that Jesus celebrated with his disciples on the evening of the Friday on which he actually was sacrificed for our sins. That is why Paul writes in 1 Corinthians 11:26: "For whenever you eat this bread and drink this cup, you proclaim the Lord's death until he comes." But our eternal salvation was made possible by the sacrifice that Jesus offered to the Father in expiation for our sins when he died on the cross once and for all, which is what is referenced as the "one sacrifice that made us perfect forever" in Hebrews 10:14b.

One other ongoing misconception about the Lord's Supper is that the full presence of Jesus is there in the consecrated bread consumed during the Lord's Supper celebration by the one who partakes of it during the Lord's Supper celebration. ***This is not supported by the Word of God as Jesus himself says in John 6:55 that his "flesh is real food and his blood is real drink" and nothing more or nothing less than that.*** In this context, it is to be noted that nowhere does it say in the Scriptures that Jesus comes into a believer when he/she partakes of the Lord's Supper; whereas in many places, we read that spiritual life is imparted to a believer when he believes in the name of Jesus, who is our Lord, Savior, and Redeemer.

Let us examine a couple of examples to illustrate this point. For example, in 2 Corinthians 13:5, Paul tells us: ***"Examine yourselves to see whether you are in the faith; test yourselves. Do you not realize that Christ Jesus is in you unless, of course, you fail the test?"*** Thus, it is clear here that when we are not in faith, Jesus Christ is not in us. Another example to illustrate this point is John 20:30–31 where we read: "Jesus did many other miraculous signs in the presence of his disciples, which are not recorded in this book. But these are written that you may believe that Jesus is the Christ, the Son of God, and that ***by believing you may have life in his name.***" Here it is also clear that it is through faith that a Christian becomes and stays a Christian.

With that said, I believe that there are two possibilities for how the teaching that there is the real presence of Jesus in the Holy Eucharist infiltrated into the teachings of the Catholic Church. One of them is John 6:53–54 where Jesus tells the disciples: "I tell you the truth, unless you eat the flesh of the Son of Man and drink his blood, you have no life in you. Whoever eats my flesh and drinks my blood has eternal life, and I will raise him up at the last day." ***Here it is clear that even though it is not either the flesh or the blood of Jesus that ignites spiritual life within a Christian, both to sustain and strengthen it, according to Jesus, it is necessary that a Christian be regularly fed with his flesh and blood!*** In other words, the bread and wine used in the Lord's Supper—which are transformed into his body and blood, respectively, when they are consecrated during the Eucharistic celebration—are necessary to nourish the spiritual life of a Christian even though spiritual life is never imparted by merely eating the consecrated bread or by drinking the consecrated blood consumed by a participant of the Lord's Supper if it is not accompanied by faith also. ***Thus, a non-Christian can never become a Christian by simply consuming the consecrated bread and wine unless he receives it after he comes to believe in Christ and thereby accepts Jesus Christ as his Savior, Redeemer, and the Lord of his life.***

A NEW PENTECOST

FOR A STARVING WORLD!

Part B
Contents

Part B

An Introduction to
The Theology of Being Born Again

Important note: **Even if you miss everything else in this book, DO NOT MISS the four steps to becoming a born-again Christian (*see the section after this Introduction*).**

A brand-new storm is brewing over the horizon; a new Pentecost is coming to all Christians—Catholics and non-Catholics alike! Yes, the Holy Spirit is taking charge of Christ's church like never before through a worldwide born-again experience that God desires for all Christians to experience! This is the fulfillment of what was prophesied in Joel 2:28–29 where God says:

> I will pour out my Spirit on all people. Your sons and daughters will prophesy, your old men will dream dreams, your young men will see visions. Even on my servants, both men and women, I will pour out my Spirit in those days… And every one who calls on the name of the LORD will be saved…

How is this going to happen? It is going to happen in two ways: either by millions of followers of Christ (around ten million or so) becoming "the most beloved children of God" as Daniel was (which is covered here in the first part of the book which is an introduction to the whole book) or by becoming a born-again Christians (which is covered in detail in the first part of the book) or through prayer rallies conducted worldwide by the Prayer Rally Ministry (which is described at the end of the book). Either way, now is the time like never before for millions of souls to be "made disciples of all nations" as Jesus commanded us to do in Matthew 28:19–20. Here Jesus said, "Therefore go and make disciples of all nations." Even though preaching the gospel and making disciples of everyone around us, both near and far, was always in season in the past, we are now in the *homestretch* days of this evangelization period. It is time to make an all-out effort to do it as though there is no tomorrow, remembering what Jesus has told us in John 9:4: "As long as it is day, we must do the work of him who sent me. Night is coming, when no one can work."

As the God-designated servant of God—the Prophet from Oklahoma City—I am convinced that just as there is a *peak ripening season* when almost all the mangoes on the tree all at the same time ripen, we are living in a time when the Holy Spirit will be poured out like *never before* by God the Father as it was prophesied by Him through the mouth of Prophet Joel in Joel 2:28–29. And I feel just as Mordecai, the uncle of Esther, felt about Esther as it is described in Esther 4:14, "And who knows but that you have come to royal position for such a time as this?" I feel that the Lord has brought me to this vintage point in time such as this for the salvation of millions and millions of souls in these last days. As we read in 1 Cor. 14:8, I have a duty to make sure that the trumpet sounds a clear call so that everyone will get ready for the battle by coming to their senses in these last days before the imminent great day of the Lord. Maybe it is only my dream!

But I do see the dream! Yes, I cannot hold back anymore! I will never rest until everyone on the planet has been made disciples either by *being born again* or by becoming a *most beloved child of God* as Daniel was! As the subject in the second part of the book is how to be born again, which is the central theme of the book, let me ask you, "What is the born-again experience that Jesus talked about in John 3:3?" Jesus said in John 3:3, "I tell you the truth: no one can enter the kingdom of God unless he is born again." Jesus explained in John 3:5, "I tell you the truth: no one can enter the kingdom of God unless he is born of water and the Spirit." Everyone is born of water when he/she is born following the rupture of the water-filled section of his/her mother's womb. I believe it is the placenta in which the baby floats around for the few days that the baby spends prior to the baby's birth. This is common to every human being. But to enter the kingdom of heaven every individual needs a second birth. This birth is the birth from the Holy Spirit. This second birth is absolutely necessary because in Jesus's own explanation in John 3:6, "Flesh gives birth to flesh, but the Spirit gives birth to spirit." Unfortunately, there are so few born-again Christians in this present-day corrupted world because sadly but truly, there may be only a handful of genuinely born-again Christians if at all there are any!

Why Is Being Born Again an Absolute Necessity to Go to Heaven

Jesus Himself gives us the answer to this question in John 6:63: "The Spirit gives life; the flesh counts for nothing. The words I have spoken to you are spirit and they are life." What does this mean? Everyone who is not born again is living in the flesh. In other words, if we compare our spiritual life to a car trip, our car is still in the garage if we are not born again. We must wake up to this reality. In this situation, action on our part cannot wait any longer! But on behalf of us, however, Jesus did something truly amazing! By one sacrifice, he offered on Calvary two thousand years ago, he made perfect forever those who are being made holy." Therefore, conditionally speaking, we are all 100 percent perfect because of what Jesus did for us on Calvary! Don't let anyone tell you otherwise!

However, even though Christ paid the penalty for our sins by dying on the cross for reinstating our relationship with God, which was lost because of Adam's sin, this relationship has to be claimed by placing our faith in Jesus Christ and believing why He did what He did on the cross for us. That is why we read in Ephesians 2:8–10, "For it is by grace you have been saved, through faith—and this not from yourselves, it is the gift of God—not by works, so that no one can boast. For we are God's workmanship, created in Christ Jesus to do good works, which God prepared in advance for us to do." Mainly we have to do two things: First of all, we are called to live up to our calling as we read in 1 Peter 2:9, "to be a chosen people, a royal priesthood, a holy nation, a people belonging to God, that you may declare the praises of him who called you out of darkness into his wonderful light." Secondly, we have to do the will of God, even as Jesus did while he was on this earth as we read in John 4:34, "My food is to do the will of him who sent me and to finish his work."

On account of the sinful nature that we are born with due to Adam's disobedience, we are all born as part of a rebellious remnant. As a result, all of us are disobedient people who do not want to submit to God's commands and counseling just as our ancestors in the Old Testament were. Thus, we read in Psalm 95:10–11:

> For forty years I was angry with that generation; I said, "they are a people whose hearts go astray, and they have not known my ways." So, I declared on oath in anger, "They shall never enter my rest."

For this situation to change, we absolutely need nothing short of a sea change in our rebellious nature. This is the only way we can be transformed into an obedient flock that will listen to our good shepherd, Jesus, and walks in his ways by "walking by faith" as God wants us to do in Psalm 32:8 to become born-again disciples of Jesus Christ! This process is explained at length in the chapter on the four step process of becoming a born-again Christian that you are reading in this book. As you may be aware, the present-day spiritual dissipation and moral decline did not happen overnight even though there was a robust outpouring of the Holy Spirit in the early history of the Church about which we read in Acts 2 through 7. The martyrdom of Stephen invigorated the faith and the Church spread out far and wide in different directions. But the persecution that the Church experienced in Acts 8 caused the church to spread to Judea, Samaria, and to the remote parts of the world. But gradually the Church pulled back and faith became weaker and weaker among the Christian churches in all denominations.

But the early Church during the time of Paul was very strong and the apostles and disciples scattered throughout the world. The primary reason for this was the zeal and intense desire of Paul to take the Gospel to the most remote parts of the world. Thus, Apostles like

Philip and Thomas went to Africa and India. The single most reason why the Gospel spread far and wide into the most remote parts of the world was that the early Apostles like Paul greatly emphasized the role of the Holy Spirit wherever they went. For example, in Acts 19:2 and elsewhere, we see Paul asking the Christians if they had received the Holy Spirit. Whenever and wherever he went, if the answer to his question was a no, he made sure that they received the Holy Spirit by laying hands on them. When he did it, immediately they received the Holy Spirit and as a visible sign, they always spoke in tongues. This was typical of what happened in the early Church during the time of Paul (Acts 19:6).

Unfortunately, during the laying of hands by the pastor or the priests in today's church denominations, including the Catholic church, I have not heard even a single instance when the recipient of the laying of hands ever spoke or praised God in tongues. This makes me wonder whether the recipients of laying hands truly and really received the Holy Spirit during the administration of the Sacrament of Confirmation or other services meant for the invocation of the Holy Spirit on the recipients. In fact, it is extremely hard for me to believe that the Holy Spirit ever descends on the recipients in these cases of laying of hands on the believers. This scenario definitely calls for a New Pentecost in our Christian circles and Christian communities.

It also screams for an answer to the question of whether such recipients are saved or not by receiving the Holy Spirit. It is high time that, like Paul, we start asking the most supreme and paramount question we should be asking Christians everywhere without regard to the circumstances in which we are. Because Christ is asking a very important truth regarding each and every Christian that we meet. It is found in Luke 9:25, "What good is it for a man to gain the whole world and yet lose or forfeit his very soul?" And if you think that in your churches or anywhere outside if you are ashamed to ask your fellow Christian this question, I have bad news for you. The bad news is that Jesus says in Luke 9:26, "If anyone is ashamed of me and my words, the Son of Man will be ashamed of him when he comes in his glory and in the glory of the Father and of the holy angels." If this question is so vitally important, as someone in his seventies, I should have been asked this question at least a couple of hundred times in my lifetime by someone who is a born-again Christian. Unfortunately, the answer is that I have been asked this question maybe a couple of times only during my entire life. As long as this is the case, I am pretty sure that our world is in dire need of a new Pentecost, which should transform us all into born-again Christians or the beloved disciples of Christ who will not be ashamed to ask the most important question that Paul always asked the Christians he met all around him.

More reasons we have an urgent need for a New Pentecost

I like to tell you about Prophet Elisha who asked Elijah, his master, for a double portion of his spirit before Elijah was taken up to heaven described in 2 Kings 2:9–10. Here we read:

> When they had crossed, Elijah said to Elisha, "Tell me, what can I do for you before I am taken from you?"
> "Let me inherit a double portion of your spirit," Elisha replied.
> "You have asked a difficult thing," Elijah said, "yet if you see me when I am taken from you, it will be yours—otherwise not."

After Elijah told Elisha that he will have a double portion of the spirit of Elijah upon his being taken up to heaven only if he witnessed Elijah's ascent into heaven, he was extremely careful to follow Elijah everywhere he went. Thus Elisha was able to see the departure of Elijah into heaven, and thus he was able to get a double portion of the spirit of Elijah, which was extremely beneficial for him to meet the challenges that he faced when he led the Israelites after the reign of Prophet Elijah. The valuable lesson that we learn from the accounts of these two prophets is that possessing the Spirit of God had proven to be of extreme importance in the lives of everyone who lived on this earth and beyond.

If there ever was a time to possess a double portion of the Spirit of God, it is now. In fact, the challenges that we are facing now in our spiritual life and physical life and those we will be facing in the coming days are so monumental that we need to be filled with the Holy Spirit to live a victorious life while we live on this earth as well as when we will be called out from this life to the next. In fact, we not only need to be filled with the Spirit, but we need to be controlled by the Spirit for us to live a successful Christian life. That is why Paul tells us in Romans 8:9, "If anyone does not have the Spirit of Christ, he does not belong to Christ." No wonder Jesus told Nicodemus in John 3:3, "Unless one is born again, he will not enter the kingdom of heaven." In Romans 8:16, we read that we are children of God only if we are controlled by the Holy Spirit on this side of eternity.

Another compelling argument for every Christian to be filled and controlled by the Holy Spirit for which we desperately need a Second Pentecost is what we read in 2 Timothy 3:1–5 as below:

> But mark this: There will be terrible times in the last days. People will be lovers of themselves, lovers of money, boastful, proud, abusive, disobedient to their parents, ungrateful, unholy, without love, unforgiving, slanderous, without self-control, brutal, not lovers of the good, treacherous, rash, conceited, lovers of pleasure rather than lovers of God—having a form of godliness but denying its power. Have nothing to do with them.

Satan knows that there is only limited time for him to lead astray the bride of Jesus Christ who are all the saints waiting for the second arrival of Jesus Christ. That is why we are being warned by the Word of God in Ephesians 6:14–18 to:

> Stand firm girdled with the belt of truth buckled around our waist, with the breastplate of righteousness in place, and with your feet fitted with

the readiness that comes from the gospel of peace. In addition to all this we are asked to take up the shield of faith with which we can extinguish all the flaming arrows of the evil one. We should then take the helmet of salvation and the sword of the Spirit which is the Word of God. And then we are asked to pray in the Spirit on all occasions with all kinds of payers and prayer requests. With this in mind, we have to be alert and always keep on praying for all the saints.

At this crucial time in which the imminent arrival of Christ, our bridegroom can happen at any time, we cannot afford to take even a single wrong step which may result in our missing our chance to meet our bridegroom. Yes, the danger is as real as it can be for our "master to come on a day when we do not expect him and an hour we are not aware of" as we are warned by Jesus Himself in Matthew 24:50. We cannot afford to take even the slightest chance to miss His coming only to be "cut into pieces and assigned a place with the hypocrites, where there will be weeping and gnashing of teeth." We should never forget that as we read in Genesis 19:26, it cost Lot's wife her very life just for looking back just once as the Lord was raining down burning sulfur on Sodom and Gomorrah out of the heavens." To drive home this very important message into the hearts and minds of our brothers and sisters, we need nothing short of a New Pentecost.

Why Did We Need Jesus to Save Us, and How Did He Do It?

Now let me explain why it was impossible for anyone to obey the commandments and thus go to heaven even before the time of Elijah and Elisha. It was impossible for anyone to completely obey the law that came to us through Moses and go to heaven because human nature had suffered such a heavy blow from the fall of Adam and Eve that humanity's sinful nature made it impossible to overcome sin with the efforts of man alone. When Jesus came with his modified version of the Ten Commandments, it was made even tougher to obey. For example, "Do not commit adultery" was modified by Jesus when He said "that anyone who looks at a woman lustfully has already committed adultery in her heart" (Matt. 5:27).

Similarly, He has modified all the laws of Moses, making them more stringent and harder to obey. It is true that Jesus condensed the entire law into two commands in Matthew 22:37–40. Here Jesus said, "Love the Lord your God with all your heart and with all your soul and with all your mind. This is the first and greatest commandment. And the second is like it: Love your neighbor as yourself. All the Law and the Prophets hang on these two commandments."

Let me ask you, is there anyone in this whole world from the time of Jesus or ever before or after Christ who has loved God with all his heart, soul, and mind? The answer is *no*. By the same token, is there anyone who has loved his neighbor as himself? Again, the answer is *no*. In fact, Jesus's *simplified version* of the law is much harder than the original Ten Commandments to obey.

Ever since the fall of man, it was impossible for anyone to obey the commandments of God to go to heaven because as we read in

Revelation 21:27, "Nothing impure will enter heaven." So, we were unable to enter heaven because none of us could achieve the level of holiness that is needed to enter heaven on our own merit. However, Jesus did something that was both unimaginable and hard even to comprehend. Thus, in John 1:12 we read, "To all who received Him, to those who believed in His name, He gave the right to become children of God." Thus, the theology of becoming born-again Christians was born. Because as we read in 2 Corinthians 1:22, "Anointed those who accepted Christ and believed in His name by setting His seal of ownership and put His Spirit in their hearts as a deposit, guaranteeing what is to come."

Thus, through the gift of the Holy Spirit, God has given us the guarantee that we will one day be in heaven as long as we become the born-again children of God now. And in order for this to happen, we also have to repent of our sins and be healed of our spiritual wounds as God promises us in Isaiah 44:22: "I have swept away your offenses like a cloud, your sins like the morning mist. Return to me, for I have redeemed you." Here, in order to accept Jesus as our redeemer, we have to acknowledge Jesus's name as our redeemer and return to Him for His forgiveness of our sins and our redemption.

But how did Jesus accomplish our redemption and salvation? Simple! Jesus liberated us from the yoke of law and put us under the law of the Spirit as we read in Romans 8:2. Here we read, "Through Jesus Christ, the law of the Spirit of life has set me free from the law of sin and death."

Again, we read about this in Galatians 5:4–6:

> You who are trying to be justified by law have been alienated from Christ; you have fallen away from grace. But by faith we eagerly await through the Spirit the righteousness for which we hope. For in Christ Jesus neither circumcision nor un-circumcision has any value. The only thing that counts is faith expressing itself through love.

What all this means is that when we believe in the name of Jesus, we also believe in all the twelve or so various names of God because Jesus is God. These twelve names include such names as Yehowah Ire (the God who provides for all our needs as and when we need them), Yehowah Raffa (the God who heals us from all our illnesses), Yehowah Shama (the God who is with us all the time), Yehowah Ershadi (the God Almighty), Yehowah Shalom (the God who is our peace), Yehowah Elohim (the God who creates), Yehowah Adonai (the God who is our Lord), Yehowah Nissi (the God who is our banner of victory), etc. When we believe in all these names of Jesus and accept Him as the Lord of our lives, He gives us the Holy Spirit as an eternal guarantee for our salvation.

Of course, at this point in our spiritual life, we are still obligated to obey all the laws and commandments, but there is a huge difference in our attitude toward obedience! Whenever we fall short of completely obeying the two commands of Jesus—the first one to love God with all our heart and soul and mind and the second to love our neighbor as ourselves—Jesus's grace covers our *performance gap*. In other words, suppose I obey the two commandments to the tune of, say, 40 percent and fail by 60 percent. The 60 percent performance gap is covered by the grace that He offers me on account of the merits of Jesus's death on the cross. Thus, when God the Father looks at my soul, it is 100 percent holy and therefore, totally acceptable to Him and thus sees the same level of righteousness and holiness that Jesus Himself possesses. Thus, I am accepted as holy by God so as to be fully qualified to enter heaven.

Suppose another believer has obeyed 50 percent instead of my 40 percent. In his case, the performance gap of 50 percent will be covered by the grace that Jesus gives him if he is a believer and accepted Jesus as his personal Lord and Savior. Thus, he is also accepted by God the Father as though he has the same level of holiness as Jesus Christ Himself, making him also worthy of eternal salvation and qualified to enter heaven. This kind of justification, made possible by the Holy Spirit who takes up residence in a born-again Christian, is what makes him worthy of heaven. This is true in spite of every type of performance gap in life in loving God wholeheartedly, whether the performance gap is 60 percent, 50 percent, 15 percent, or even 10 percent. Sounds like an easy and perfect plan for anyone and everyone to enter heaven with ease! Then why is it that the Christian life today is such a struggle and going to heaven such a lifelong battle? There are two reasons which we are going to examine here.

The Enemy Is Strong,
So We Need Strong Weapons

The first reason is what Jesus said in John 10:10 where we read, "The thief comes only to steal and kill and destroy; I have come that they may have life and have it to the full." Yes, on the one side, we have Jesus who offers us an abundant life, who is lavishing on us grace over and beyond what we need. But on the other side, our archenemy, "the devil is prowling around like a roaring lion looking for someone to devour. Resist him, standing firm in the faith, because you know that your brothers throughout the world are undergoing the same kind of sufferings" (1 Pet. 5:8–9).

As the children of God, we have let our guards down since we have underestimated the power and influence of the devils under the leadership of Satan. As a result, even though in Ephesians 6:10–18 we have been warned to stay alert and fit for our ongoing battle with Satan and his devils, we let our guards down, and thus, we have been sometimes routed by the evil forces under the leadership of Satan. In Ephesians 6:10–18 we read:

> Finally, be strong in the Lord and in his mighty power. Put on the full armor of God so that you can take your stand against the devil's schemes. For our struggle is not against flesh and blood, but against the rulers, against the authorities, against the powers of this dark world and against the spiritual forces of evil in the heavenly realms. Therefore, put on the full armor of God, so that when

the day of evil comes, you may be able to stand your ground, and after you have done everything, to stand. Stand firm then, with the belt of truth buckled around your waist, with the breastplate of righteousness in place, and with your feet fitted with the readiness that comes from the gospel of peace. In addition to all this, take up the shield of faith, with which you can extinguish all the flaming arrows of the evil one. Take the helmet of salvation and the sword of the Spirit, which is the Word of God. And pray in the Spirit on all occasions with all kinds of prayers and requests. With this in mind, be alert and always keep on praying for all the saints.

Jesus Had the Perfect Plan, but We Need a Helper to Execute It!

As Paul tells us in the above passage, we have failed to be strong in the Lord and in his mighty power and wear all the full armor of God to stand up against Satan and his satanic forces behind him. As we are instructed to do in 1 Peter 5:6, we have failed to "humble ourselves under God's mighty hand, that he may lift us up in due time." Jesus's plan to take every one of us to heaven was by making us all born-again Christians, and it was a perfect plan. That is why He made this very clear to Nicodemus in John 3:3 as we saw above. But no matter how good the plan is, it will work only if we follow up on it and stay with it. Let me illustrate what I mean by an example from my own life.

A Work Plan Will Succeed Only When the One Who Tests the Plan Obeys All the Rules

About forty-five years ago, in the year 1997, I wrote a book titled *Reflex Typing Theory: A New Way to Improve Typing Skills.* I was 100 percent sure that this is a theory that works if someone was really serious about improving his typing speed. My confidence was based on my own firsthand experience in improving my own typing speed using this method. About two years prior to the writing of this book, I had proved to myself that this theory and method really worked. Without keeping you, the readers of this book, in suspense, let me give you a definition of RTT. The theory of RTT says that "an office worker's typing speed can be dramatically increased by simulating an actual typing session in which randomly selected words are *mentally typed* by imagining one's hands and fingers to be above the keyboard of a computer or a typewriter and moving the fingers of both the hands as closely as possible to resemble an actual typing session." The reason why this experiment works to improve one's typing speed is that in this simulation of typing, there is a sound logic of repeated reinforcement being implemented to develop a *reflex action* for the fingers of both hands as the brain is contemplating a word to be typed.

In the above example, it is the repeated reinforcement of a physical action accompanying a mental exercise that enables the skill of typing to become faster and faster through a reflex that is being developed in which both the brain and the fingers participate in a coordinated exercise between the two. Now what I am trying to say here is this: I wrote this book and tried to sell copies of this book at a very reasonable price of $15.00 per copy. But I was able to sell only about fifteen copies, and therefore, as you can tell, I was disappointed.

But I kept on practicing RTT for my personal edification and because I had high expectations that the ability to type really fast will someday enable me to land a clerical job first and then a bright career path using my high typing skill, which I knew I was well on my way of fast developing. So, I had no time to get discouraged about not selling any significant copies of my book on RTT. How right I was! When I initially started practicing typing using RTT as my only typing exercise to improve my typing skills, my typing speed was in the neighborhood of twenty-five words per minute or so. But my typing speed steadily increased going from twenty-five to thirty-five to forty-two to fifty, etc. Within a couple of years, I was able to get a clerk typist position at a printing shop engaged in typesetting business. Much more than speed, in typesetting, accuracy was extremely important because after a typesetting job is entered on a typesetter and the text for printing is printed on to a photographic film, the typeset copy of the text for printing was proofread for accuracy. If there is a typo, fixing the error took a lot of time. To make a long story short, even though I joined as a new employee, I became the favorite employee in the organization of about eight typesetters or so. Every year I got raises in pay, and soon, within two years or so, my hourly pay was more than that of the supervisor who had been with that typesetting company for more than fifteen years or so. I was very happy with my steady climb on the career ladder. After a handful of years in Chicago, I moved to Dallas.

Because of my typing speed of eighty-five words per minute with only two errors within a five-minute typing test, I was easily able to get into a clerk typist position, and within a year, I got into HR. Using my education degree and business degree combined with my excellent typing skill of being able to type at eighty-five words per minute, I moved through the ranks within the City of Dallas, and I had a great career in human resources. With the skills I picked up in the field of human resources, after nearly twenty years with the City of Dallas, I was hired by the federal government where I stayed about fifteen years and then retired.

The point I am trying to drive home to you is an important truth that even though I did not sell more than fifteen copies of my book on RTT, since it is a theory that really worked, it gave me a boost in my career life that I couldn't even imagine without the assistance of the idea of RTT to develop my typing skills, which really put me on a smooth career path.

Now let me tell you why I elaborated on all these experiences I went through. I learned a truth that works similarly in our spiritual world. This is probably more applicable to the truth that Jesus told Nicodemus than anything else. Even though Jesus talked so emphatically about the absolute need to be born again to enter the kingdom of heaven, unfortunately, even among the apostles, only Paul seems to have wholeheartedly embraced this most important theology applicable to every Christian's life without exception.

Just as I said in the case of my efforts to promote and sell my book, the fact that just because a certain truth is not well received by others, it does not take away anything from its immense value or its relevance to our everyday living, nor does it make its far-reaching consequences any less disastrous either with respect to its severity or its eternally crushing longevity. To put it in a nutshell, there is no loss greater than a Christian missing out on paradise. No wonder Jesus said in Luke 9:25, "What good is it for a man to gain the whole world, and yet lose or forfeit his very self?" Jesus said this in another way which puts this tragedy in perspective with regard to Judas Iscariot who betrayed Jesus. He said, "It would have been better had he not been born at all."

Only Paul Strictly Followed
the Plan of God Making
Everyone a Born-Again Christian

On the positive side, Paul, who totally embraced the theology of regeneration of a Christian that Jesus shared with Nicodemus, has a success story to tell even though no one else among the apostles shared this passion the way Paul did. The result was that only Paul could make a confident claim, as he does in 1 Corinthians 4:15 when writing to the Corinthians: "Even though you have ten thousand guardians in Christ, you do not have many fathers, for in Christ Jesus I became your father through the gospel. Therefore, I urge you to imitate me." Thus, we see that apart from Jesus, Paul was the only disciple who was absolutely sure that he was well on his way to heaven because he was the only one who was born again, as he used to ask his fellow Christians wherever he went the two all too important questions: (1) "Have you received the Holy Spirit" (Acts 19:2) and (2) "Do you have Christ in you?"

According to Jesus, only those who could answer "Yes" to these two questions would only enter the kingdom of God. Because only such Christians are born again based on what Jesus told Nicodemus. Paul was focused on making sure that this was true with every disciple that he met. Even though all Christians he came across believed in Jesus, most of them were not born again because the other apostles were not keen on asking the above two crucial questions to their believers. We see this in the fact that none of the other apostles asked their followers to imitate them in their way of living out the faith as Paul did" (Philippians 3:17).

When you come to think of it, I believe that somehow to some extent, I share the passion of Paul to see that my fellow Christians are born-again Christians. And I have often wondered why is it that the Lord has chosen me to be entrusted with this awesome ministry. First, I thought probably this must have been the sheer mercy of God behind His selecting me for this noble mission because in 2 Corinthians 4:1 Paul himself writes, "Since through God's mercy we have this ministry, we do not lose heart." But then I found out that it could be another reason also besides God's mercy on my behalf. It sounds just like the Lord Jesus, who is faithful toward those who show faithfulness toward Him and His Word, as we see in 2 Timothy 2:12–13, "If we endure, we will also reign with him. If we disown him, he will also disown us. If we are faithless, he will remain faithful, for he cannot disown himself." *A great promise of His faithfulness!*

Notice that the Word of God says, "If we endure with Him in His sufferings, we will reign with Him." Almost twenty-five years ago, I made a commitment to taste and see how faithful Jesus is in His promises. So for this purpose, I took up a great challenge to see if His promise in John 10:34–35 will come true. So I started spending an hour to an hour and a half every day until today because I wanted to be like Him. Yeah, to this day, first of all, I discovered the treasure house that the Word of God is. I found out that when I tried to be filled with the Word of God, I started becoming more and more like Him and more and more like Paul, who has been my role model ever since October 1997. I discovered that His faithfulness was beyond imagination! How else would I, a worthless creature, not only be born again in my experimentation to see if John 10:34–35 would come true in my life, but the **Lord even showed me a four-step formula to share with others who also want to become born-again Christians, something that He didn't even reveal to Paul!**

Another truth that God revealed to me about the faithfulness of Jesus is what we read above in 2 Timothy 2:13: "If we are faithless, he will remain faithful!" An example of this is Peter who denied Jesus three times, but Jesus still reinstated him (John 21:15–19) and made him the head of the church.

Becoming a Born-Again Christian Is the Greatest Blessing Ever!

To realize how great the joy of being born again is and the Holy Spirit indwelling within us, just look at what David says in Psalm 51:11–12 when he committed the sin of adultery and temporarily lost the joy of salvation! Here he says, "Do not cast me from your presence or take your Holy Spirit from me. Restore to me the joy of your salvation and grant me a willing spirit, to sustain me." David was in danger of losing the Holy Spirit who was on him! His grief and misery he experienced in his soul and body after losing the joy of salvation following his sin, which he hid for more than a year or so without confessing it to God, are described by David in Psalm 32. For example, in Psalm 32:3–4 he says, "When I kept silent, my bones wasted away through my groaning all day long. For day and night your hand was heavy upon me; my strength was sapped as in the heat of summer." If David felt so awful when he lost the joy of salvation due to his sin, how much misery and grief will we experience when we are in sin and thus lose the fellowship of the Holy Spirit **who actually resides within us—a heavenly bliss only a born-again Christian can experience?**

By the way, the difference between the grief experienced by David when he sinned was nowhere near the grief and anxiety a Christian who is born again experiences. The difference between the joy of salvation experienced by David and that experienced by a born-again Christian is huge. This is so because in the Old Testament, when the Holy Spirit came on somebody, the Holy Spirit literally came *on* that person. But in the New Testament, when a Christian is born again, the Holy Spirit comes

into the inside **of that Christian on a scale that is impossible to compare to the scale the Holy Spirit used to come *on* a person in the Old Testament.** Just for distinguishing between the two, if we describe the scale of the coming of the Holy Spirit on a person in the Old Testament as *shallow* as in the case of David or Samson or anyone else, we should describe the coming of the Holy Spirit into the inside of a born-again Christian at least as *infinitely superior*.

This difference was huge because it was in the New Testament ONLY where a believer could become a *disciple of Christ*, which was not possible in the Old Testament. **No wonder Jesus said in Luke 6:40, "A student is not above his teacher, but everyone who is fully trained will be like his teacher."** In this context, it is good to see the purpose of the calling of a Christian in the New Testament as we see it described by Paul in his prayer found in Ephesians 1:18–19: "I pray that the eyes of your heart may be enlightened in order that you may know the hope to which he has called you, the riches of his glorious inheritance in the saints, and his incomparably great power for us who believe."

If Christ Does All the Heavy Lifting, Why Should We Struggle in Our Spiritual Life?

If the hope to which He has called you are the riches of His glorious inheritance in the saints and His incomparably great power for us who believe which we just read at the end of the previous chapter, you may ask, "Why should I struggle so much to reduce my *performance gap* by becoming more and more diligent in doing the Lord's work in my life?" There are four reasons why we should struggle.

Firstly, if we are not diligent in doing the Lord's work, we may be rejected by Christ according to what we read in Revelation 3:15–16. Here we read, "Because you are lukewarm—neither hot or cold, I am about to spit you out of my mouth." In other words, if we are not fervent in the Lord's work as we are commanded to be in Romans 12:11–21, we may lose our salvation. In this context, it is worth remembering that even Paul, the most revered apostle of Jesus Christ, had great anxiety and apprehensions about himself being rejected when being judged for his merits to enter heaven. Thus, we read Paul saying in 1 Corinthians 9:25–27:

> Everyone who competes in the games goes into strict training. They do it to get a crown that will not last; but we do it to get a crown that will last forever. Therefore, I do not run like a man running aimlessly; I do not fight like a man beating the air. No, I beat my body and make it my slave

so that after I have preached to others, I myself
will not be disqualified for the prize.

Secondly, our reward in heaven will depend on how hard we
work for the Lord while we're here on earth. Thus, we read in 2 Corinthians 5:9–10, "We make it our goal to please him whether we are
at home in the body or away from it. For we must all appear before
the judgment seat of Christ that each may receive what is due him for
the things done while in the body, whether good or bad."

So, we should work as hard as possible with all the resources we
have at our disposal to bring maximum glory to God through our
hard work. Unfortunately, we are living in a Christian world where
we give a lot of undue importance to what others think or say about
us even if what they say is against the Word of God. For example, Peter once did this once as we read in Matthew 16:21–23. Here we read:

> From that time on Jesus began to explain to
> his disciples that he must go to Jerusalem and suf-
> fer many things at the hands of the elders, chief
> priests and teachers of the law, and that he must
> be killed and on the third day be raised to life.
> Peter took him aside and began to rebuke him.
> "Never, Lord," he said. "This shall never happen
> to you!" Jesus turned and said to Peter, "Get be-
> hind me, Satan! You are a stumbling block to me;
> you do not have in mind the things of God, but
> the things of men."

I once had this experience myself when I was attending the Syro-
Malabar Church Convention in Houston, Texas, USA. As many of
you may be aware of, I say "Praise the Lord" at least once during or at
the end of the homily of the Mass when I attend the church service
on Sundays. As usual, I did this during the solemn Mass on August
2, 2019. But the response from the Syro-Malabar hierarchy was totally surprising and downright reprehensible in my opinion. To my

surprise, within ten minutes after I said, "Praise the Lord" during the homily, the security guard on the premises came into the convention hall and sat by me on the left. So I was sandwiched between my wife on the right and the security guard on my left. Five minutes after he sat by me, the security guard asked me if I would step out of the hall to come outside as he wanted to have a chat with me. I came out and he asked me if I would stop chanting "Praise the Lord" during the homily. His concern was that somebody may complain about my "Praise the Lord."

My argument was that the Word of God states in Psalm 119:175, "I live for the purpose of praising God and that it is the Word of God that sustains me and nothing else." I told him that "even if he cuts off my head, my head will go on chanting 'Praise the Lord.'" In other words, I would NEVER stop praising my Lord and Savior Jesus Christ because in Psalm 34:1, we are commanded to always extol the Lord and to have His praise all the time on our lips. So the one who is in me prevailed over the one in the world who is none other than Satan himself, just as it happened when Peter tried to deter Jesus from going to the cross by rebuking Jesus not to do that. To tell you the truth, I have never felt better in my life than on that day when I boldly witnessed for Jesus Christ!

Thirdly, we have been created by God to be filled to the measure of all the fullness of God. This is what we read in Ephesians 3:16–19 where Paul prays for the believers in Ephesus. Here we read, "I pray that you, being rooted and established in love, may have power, together with all the saints, to grasp how wide and long and high and deep is the love of Christ, and to know this love that surpasses knowledge—that you may be filled to the measure of all the fullness of God."

Again, we read in Colossians 1:28–29, "We proclaim him, admonishing and teaching everyone with all wisdom, so that we may present everyone perfect in Christ. To this I labor, struggling with all his energy, which so powerfully works in me." Then again in John 15:5, "Apart from me, you can do nothing." So the choice is clear here. Either you can do all things according to what God wants us to do to bring others to the fullness of God or you can do nothing.

What makes all the difference is whether a Christian is a born-again Christian or not. If he is, he will give himself fully to the service of the Lord; if he is not, he will only be a *part-time* Christian. If we are only part-time Christians, we are not born-again Christians at all!

> For the above reasons we are commanded to be strong in the Lord and in His mighty power. Put on the full armor of God so that you can take your stand against the devil's schemes. For our struggle is not against flesh and blood, but against the rulers, against the authorities, against the powers of this dark world and against the spiritual forces of evil in the heavenly realms.

Therefore, put on the full armor of God so that when the day of evil comes, you may be able to stand your ground; and after you have done everything, to stand (Eph. 6:10–13). After all, according to the Word of God, only one-third of the angels fell and joined with Lucifer, the leader of those angels who rebelled against God. Thus, for every devil who fights against us in our spiritual battles, there are two angels who fight on our side. But God, who is above all the angels good and bad, is on our side when we stand for God and His kingdom. And He is always ready to help us and strengthen us through the Word of God and the various gifts of the Holy Spirit that God gives us to prepare us for our spiritual battles! The only thing God requires of us is that we should become born-again Christians and be diligent in our Christian living to live a life of holiness and also to "proclaim Christ, admonishing and teaching everyone with all wisdom, so that we may present everyone perfect in Christ." In attaining this second goal, Paul is our greatest example as we read in Colossians 1:28–29 above.

Benefits of Living According to the Prompting of the Holy Spirit

When we live by the prompting of the Holy Spirit, which is how every born-again Christian should and will live, we will be able to accomplish many achievements in our lives, some of which are as follows.

First, we read in 2 Corinthians 4:16, "Even though outwardly we are wasting away, we become transformed from our old self into a new self-day by day." This new self is nothing short of the likeness of God Himself as the Holy Spirit who is transforming us thin this way is the third person of the Holy Trinity. How this is being achieved is explained in Ephesians 3:16–19 where we find one of the prayers of Paul on behalf of those who live in the Spirit. Here we read:

> I pray that out of his glorious riches he may strengthen you with power through his Spirit in your inner being, so that Christ may dwell in your hearts through faith. And I pray that you, being rooted and established in love may have power together with all the saints, to grasp how wide and long and high and deep is the love of Christ, and to know this love that surpasses knowledge—that you may be filled to the measure of all the fullness of God.

In other words, when we live by the Spirit, we become more and more like God!

Secondly, we become the children of God who eventually become so strong spiritually that as we read in 1 John 3:9, we become innocent and blameless in the eyes of God, who thus gain the ability to live without sin. In 1 John 3:9 we read, "No one who is born of God will continue to sin, because God's seed remains in him; he cannot go on sinning because he has been born of God." Here notice the two expressions of action: "no one who is born of God will continue to sin" and "he cannot go on sinning."

This calls for an explanation. Just as a running fan does not immediately come to a complete halt when it is turned off, our tendency to sin may linger for a couple of days or weeks in our soul after we are born again. However, the driving force within the soul is switched from flesh-driven to Spirit-driven; thus, the appetite that used to be bent toward satisfying the flesh is suddenly changed toward satisfying the Holy Spirit who is now in control. Thus, it is a new orientation within the soul of the born-again Christian being initiated and controlled by the Holy Spirit. That is why 1 John 3:9 says that "no one who is born of God will continue to sin, because God's seed remains in him; he cannot go on sinning because he has been born of God."

This can be explained with a perfect example from nature. We all know that a mango tree can only produce mangoes, and apple tree can produce only apples. Now I ask you to use some imagination. I know it is impossible to do this in the world of plants and trees, but all the same, I am going to ask you to imagine it anyway. Suppose you were successful in changing the genetic composition of a mango tree and now what used to be a mango tree has become an apple tree, just like any other apple tree that we see around us. Imagine that this transformation is complete and irreversible. Now no matter how hard the mango tree tries to produce mangoes, which it used to produce before, it cannot produce mangoes because there has been a total and irreversible transformation of the tree from a mango tree into an apple tree. Here, *total and irreversible* means that the whole mango tree—including its trunk, branches, and even the root system— have been changed in its entirety. If we imagine the mango tree as a sinful man before he was born again to become the apple tree and the apple tree as the transformed born-again man who used to be the mango tree before the transformation, we can see clearly that the roots of the mango tree have now been transformed into the roots of the apple tree. If we consider the roots of the mango tree to be the source of all the sinful thoughts and sinful deeds, once again imagining the mango tree as the sinful man before he became a born-again Christian, we can see that because of the transformation of the root system. Such sinful thoughts and sinful deeds have also been transformed to match the thoughts and deeds of a born-again Christian who cannot sin according to John (1 John 3:9) and John (1 John 5:18) from the verses quoted below. When a Christian is born again, an identical change occurs as John says here in 1 John 3:9 or as John says in 1 John 5:18 that anyone born of God does not continue to sin because the one who was born of God keeps him safe, and the evil one cannot harm him."

And just as it is impossible for a human body to enter heaven as Paul tells us in 1 Corinthians 15:50, by the same token, it is impossible for a sinful soul to enter heaven also according to what we read in Revelation 21:8. Here we read, "The cowardly, the unbelieving, the vile, the murderers, the sexually immoral, those who practice magic arts, the idolaters and all liars—their place will be in the fiery lake of burning sulfur." That is why Jesus said to Nicodemus in John 3:5, "I tell you the truth, no one can enter the kingdom of God unless he is born of water and the Spirit." And the reason is that one who is born again is without sin because he cannot sin as we read in 1 John 3:9.

Thirdly, we will be able to experience full freedom in Christ with a 100 percent guarantee that we will one day be with Christ face-to-face which will last for all of eternity. This is the meaning of what we read in Romans 8:2, "Through Christ Jesus the law of the Spirit of life set me free from the law of sin and death." When we are born again, any and all laws that deal with sin have no impact on us because we live under the law of the Spirit, which is based on love, faith, and grace. We come under this law when we are born again. And "there is no fear in love. But perfect love drives out fear, because fear has to do with punishment. The one who fears is not made perfect in love." We are made perfect in love when we are born again, and therefore, when we become born-again Christians, we don't have to fear anything because God gives us a guarantee as we are made firm in Christ. That is why we read in 2 Corinthians 1:20–22:

> For no matter how many promises God has made, they are all "Yes" in Christ. And so, through him the "Amen" is spoken by us to the glory of God. Now it is God who makes both us and you stand firm in Christ. He anointed us, set his seal of ownership on us, and put his Spirit in our hearts as a deposit, guaranteeing what is to come.

Here the reference "what is to come" is a reference to *eternal life*. Therefore, we have a guarantee by God Himself that we will be admitted to heaven when we die because God the Father makes this assurance when we are born again, and the Holy Spirit that He gives to us when we are born again is an ironclad guarantee that we will be admitted into heaven upon our death.

The above guarantee is further explained in Romans 8:13–17 where we read:

> If you live according to the sinful nature, you will die; but if by the Spirit you put to death the misdeeds of the body, you will live because those who are led by the Spirit of God are sons of God. For you did not receive a spirit that makes you a slave again to fear, but you received the Spirit of sonship. And by him we cry, "Abba, Father."
>
> The Spirit himself testifies with our spirit that we are God's children. Now if we are children, then we are heirs—heirs of God and co-heirs with Christ, if indeed we share in his sufferings in order that we may also share in his glory.

Fourthly, when we are born again, we experience complete peace and joy which the world cannot take away from us because the peace that Jesus gives us is entirely different from the peace that the world gives to us, which is temporary and does not last (John 14:27). In John 15:7–8, Jesus further reassures us, "If you remain in me and my words remain in you, ask whatever you wish, and it will be given you. This is to my father's glory, that you bear much fruit, showing yourselves to be my disciples." In fact, when we become a born-again Christians, we will be producing the nine fruits of the Holy Spirit described in Galatians 5:22. These are: love, joy, peace, patience, kindness, goodness, faithfulness, gentleness, and self-control.

Fifth and lastly, when we are born again, we can live a sinless life. Some Christian denominations are so hooked up to going for confession to a priest to obtain remission for their members. But once we are born again, we can still go for confession, but we don't have to if we have been genuinely born again. It is because as we read in 1 John 3:9, a born-again Christian cannot sin, and therefore, there is no need for him to go for confession. This point is further reinforced in 1 John 5:18 where John once again tells us, "We know that anyone born of God **does not continue to sin**; the one who was born of God keeps him safe, and the evil one cannot harm him."

What Are the Four Steps to Become a Born-Again Christian?

Jesus said in John 3:3, "I tell you the truth, no one can see the kingdom of God unless he is born again." Because [until then], "All you Do in the Flesh Counts for Nothing" (John 6:63).

As an introduction to the theology and practice of how a Christian can be born again, I would like to point out that this Holy Spirit-inspired method of a Christian becoming a born-again Christian has not come easy for me. This is the result of a twenty-five-year- old study and a personal experiment that started on October 27, 1997, and continues to this very day as of April 15, 2023. What triggered this long journey was an unquenchable thirst that the Holy Spirit twenty-five years ago put in my heart. It happened when I read John 10:34–35, which talks about the conversation that Jesus had with the Pharisees. Here we read about Jesus asking the Pharisees, "Is it not written in your Law, 'I have said you are gods'? If he called them 'gods' to whom the Word of God came—and the Scripture cannot be broken…"

In a nutshell, the Holy Spirit spoke to me in the same way that Jesus talked to the Pharisees; that if the Word of God comes to someone in a significant and meaningful way so as to make a big impact, he or she will become like God. I was convinced that if I can become like God, there is nothing better than that for me to achieve in my life. Therefore, I took up the challenge to experiment and see if such a transformation can be made a reality in my life. Thus, my spiritual journey began on October 27, 1997, and passed through many twists and turns with many messages the Holy Spirit gave me which I am sharing here in this book.

The personal challenge that I took upon myself almost twenty-five years ago may seem just an isolated incident to you. But in the context of the coronavirus pandemic that is plaguing the world today, (April 15, 2023), the Holy Spirit has revealed to me that like Queen Esther in the Bible, God has been preparing me for "such a time as this" (Esther 4:14) since the call of our risen Christ more than two thousand years ago to "go and make disciples of all nations" (Matt. 28:19) has gone unheeded for the most part in today's "crooked and depraved" world (Phil. 2:15). This in spite of the awesome "emancipation declaration" that Jesus made when He read from the passage in Isaiah 61:1–3 at the start of His ministry. On that day, when He entered the synagogue and the Scriptures were given to Him to read, He was given the scroll of the prophet Isaiah to read from. He read from the scroll and said:

> The Spirit of the Sovereign Lord is on me, because the Lord has anointed me to preach good news to the poor.
>
> He has sent me to bind up the brokenhearted, to proclaim freedom for the captives and release from darkness for the prisoners,
>
> To proclaim the year of the Lord's favor and the day of vengeance of our God, to comfort all who mourn,
>
> And provide for those who grieve in Zion— to bestow on them a crown of beauty instead of ashes, the oil of gladness instead of mourning, and a garment of praise instead of a spirit of despair.
>
> They will be called oaks of righteousness, a planting of the Lord for the display of His splendor.

Since the Christian world has not taken the command of Jesus to offer the gospel in a meaningful and significant scale anywhere close to what He had in mind, I believe He has appointed me to fill the void. And therefore, without a whole lot of introduction, I am presenting here the four steps to become a born-again Christian. Jesus Himself was filled with the Holy Spirit on the day of His baptism from John the Baptist as described in Acts 3:13–17 just before He started His ministry. After a few weeks into His ministry, He once again tried to impart the same Holy Spirit who came down upon Him to His disciples while conversing with Nicodemus, His secret disciple to whom He said in John 3:3, "I tell you the truth, no one can see the kingdom of God unless he is born again." This was the second round of the descent of the Holy Spirit culminating on the day of Pentecost about which we read in Acts 2:1–4. Now the disciples were all baptized with the Holy Spirit and the church began growing.

How Did the Disciples Deviate from Teaching about Being Born Again?

As we read in Acts 19:2, it was the custom of the disciples to ask the believers wherever they went if they received the Holy Spirit to become born-again Christians. When they answered and said that they had not even heard about the Holy Spirit, Paul told them that it was important for them to believe in Jesus to receive the Holy Spirit. Then he placed his hands on them and the Holy Spirit came on them, and they spoke in tongues and prophesied. There were about twelve of them there in Ephesus who thus received the Holy Spirit (Acts 19:7). Thus, it became a tradition for the early apostles to talk to their future disciples to find out if they had received the Holy Spirit and anoint them by placing their hands over them to administer the baptism of the Holy Spirit to them whenever they came across disciples who had not received the Holy Spirit.

This practice went on for years and centuries. But somewhere along the history of the church, the church slipped away from the practice of making sure that the believers received the Holy Spirit to become the kind of disciples that Jesus had envisioned and dreamed of. Probably, this was the greatest trick of Satan to destroy the church as he has always done to distract the church from following the promptings of the Holy Spirit as the Word of God commands all churches to follow in the book of Revelation. Or perhaps the churches have become accustomed to ignoring the most repeated message to raise the bar on giving fully to the work of the Lord (1 Cor. 15:58) or any of the highest standards of excellence (Phil. 4:8–9). Here Paul tells us:

"Finally, brothers, whatever is true, whatever is noble, whatever is right, whatever is pure, whatever is lovely, whatever is admirable—if anything is excellent or praiseworthy—think about such things. Whatever you have learned or received or heard from me, or seen in me—put it into practice. And the God of peace will be with you."

Or once again, perhaps the reason for the falling away of the church may have been that we have neglected to attain the higher standards in the essential elements of the Christian virtues in the various aspects of the abundant Christian living in accordance with what we have been advised to do in 2 Peter 1:5–11. Here we read:

"Make every effort to add to your faith goodness, and to goodness, knowledge; and to knowledge, self-control; and to self-control, perseverance; and to perseverance, godliness, and to godliness, brotherly kindness, and to brotherly kindness, love. For if you possess these qualities in increasing measure, they will keep you from being ineffective and unproductive in your knowledge of our Lord Jesus Christ. But if anyone does not have them, he is nearsighted and blind, and has forgotten that he has been cleansed from his past sins. Therefore, my brothers, be all the more eager to make your calling and election sure. For if you do these things, you will never fall, and you will receive a rich welcome into the eternal kingdom of our Lord and Savior Jesus Christ."

Yet another possibility may be that we have lowered the bar on godliness in our lives both in our word and in action in total disregard for what we have been asked to do in Jude 14–16. Here we read:

"Enoch, the seventh from Adam, prophesied about these men: "See, the Lord is coming with thousands upon thousands of his holy ones to judge everyone, and to convict all the ungodly of all the ungodly acts they have done in the ungodly way, and of all the harsh words ungodly sinners have spoken against him." These men are grumblers and faultfinders; they follow their own evil desires; they boast about themselves and flatter others for their own advantage."

Or perhaps the falling away of the church through the centuries may have been due to the lack of restraints our early ancestors may have failed to exert in living a holy life as we read in Jude 5–8. Here we read:

"Though you already know all this, I want to remind you that the Lord delivered his people out of Egypt, but later destroyed those who did not believe. And the angels who did not keep their positions of authority but abandoned their own home—these he has kept in darkness, bound with everlasting chains for judgment on the great Day. In a similar way, Sodom and Gomorrah and the surrounding towns gave themselves up to sexual immorality and perversion. They serve as an example of those who suffer the punishment of eternal fire."

In the very same way, these dreamers pollute their own bodies, reject authority and slander celestial beings. But even the archangel Michael, when he was disputing with the devil about the body of Moses, did not dare to bring a slanderous accusation against him, but said, "The Lord rebuke you!" Yet these men speak abusively against whatever they do not understand; and what things they do understand by instinct, like unreasoning animals—these are the very things that destroy them.

Or perhaps the church may have slipped away from the basic threshold command of listening to the Holy Spirit in its walk as each of the seven churches was commanded to do:

- As in Revelation 2:1–7 to the church in Ephesus: "He who has an ear, let him hear what the Spirit says to the churches. To him who overcomes, I will give the right to eat from the tree of life, which is in the paradise of God."
- Or as in Revelation 2:8–11 to the church in Smyrna: "He who has an ear, let him hear what the Spirit says to the churches. He who overcomes will not be hurt at all by the second death."
- Or as in Revelation 2:12–17 to the church in Pergamum: "He who has an ear, let him hear what the Spirit says to the churches. To him who overcomes, I will give some of the hidden manna. I will also give him a white stone with a new name written on it, known only to him who receives it."
- Or as in Revelation 2:18–29 to the church in Thyatira: "To him who overcomes and does my will to the end, I will give authority over the nations—'He will rule them with an iron scepter; he will dash them to pieces like pottery'— just as I have received authority from my Father. I will also give him the morning star. He who has an ear, let him hear what the Spirit says to the churches."
- Or as in Revelation 3:1–6 to the church in Sardis: "He who overcomes will, like them, be dressed in white. I will never blot out his name from the book of life, but will acknowledge his name before Father and his angels. He who has an ear, let him hear what the Spirit says to the churches."

- Or as in Revelation 3:7–13 to the church in Philadelphia: "Him who overcomes I will make a pillar in the temple of my God. Never again will he leave it. I will write on him the name of my God and the name of the city of my God, the new Jerusalem, which is coming down out of heaven from my God; and I will also write on him my new name. He who has an ear, let him hear what the Spirit says to the churches.

- "And as in Revelation 3:14–22 to the church in Laodicea: "To him who overcomes, I will give the right to sit with me on my throne, just as I overcame and sat down with my Father on his throne. He who has an ear, let him hear what the Spirit says to the churches."

All the above seven churches had some deficiencies to overcome (except the church in Philadelphia) which the Holy Spirit pointed out to them in the individual messages to each of the seven churches, namely Ephesus, Smyrna, Pergamum, Thyatira, Sardis, and Laodicea. The disobediences and violations which occurred in each of these seven churches must have surely and definitely contributed to the spiritual decadence of our century. But based on what Jesus said to Nicodemus during the discourse He had with him, Jesus made one thing absolutely clear to him and to us in John 3:3 when He said, "I tell you the truth, no one can enter the kingdom of God unless he is born of water and the Spirit. Flesh gives birth to flesh, but the Spirit gives birth to spirit. You should not be surprised at my saying, 'You must be born again.'"

The logic here in what Jesus said to Nicodemus is crystal clear: to obey what the Spirit says to each of the seven churches and thus overcome the deficiency pointed out by the Spirit in each of the seven churches was a prerequisite to receiving the promise that each of the above churches was given. And to hear the voice of the Spirit and thus discern what was commanded to each of the churches, these churches should all have the Holy Spirit ministering in them. And to have the Holy Spirit in each of the members belonging to each of the seven churches, each member must be born again as Jesus made it clear to Nicodemus in John 3:3.

The current condition in the church of Jesus Christ is such that to ask someone if he has the Holy Spirit in him (Acts 19:2) is offensive to him. So is asking someone if he is in the faith (2 Cor. 13:5). But in the beginning years and decades and centuries of the church, asking these two questions to anyone and everyone who claimed to be a Christian was the standard practice as we read in Acts 19:2 and 2 Corinthians 13:5. Not only was it a standard practice, but it was also absolutely necessary, and the most basic requirement to be a Christian. But now that asking these two questions to any Christian is offensive, it clearly gives us the clue to the two reasons why the church of Jesus Christ today has become disqualified from being a genuine Christian church and its members from entering heaven.

Why Is It Critical for a Believer to Become a Born-Again Christian?

Let us analyze this condition of today's church a little further. In Romans 8:9 we read that "he who does not have the Spirit of Christ does not belong to Christ." Thus, he is not a Christian in any meaningful sense. So, also, is a "Christian" who does not have Christ in him because there is no Holy Spirit apart from Christ. Thus, as 2 Corinthians 13:5 says, if a Christian does not have a strong faith, Christ is not living in him and by that token, he does not belong to Christ either, which means that he is not a Christian either. Thus, authoritatively, we are able to say that the root cause for the present crisis that has resulted in our spiritual bankruptcy as a church all around the world is that we have utterly failed to exercise diligence in making sure that Jesus's topmost priority of keeping our faith strong and our spiritual fervor burning and vibrant is realized. So much so that in our church assemblies and evangelical circles, no one asks any longer, "Have you received the Holy Spirit?" This was the first question that a preacher always asked a believer as we read in Acts 19:2. Now it is almost an insult to ask this question to any of our fellow Christians. It is also an equally insulting question to ask anyone of our fellow Christians, "Have you examined to see whether you are in the faith?" (2 Cor. 13:5). But in the early centuries of Christianity, asking these two questions was as common as greeting others by saying, "Good morning" or "Good evening."

Under these gloomy conditions in which the church of Jesus Christ is languishing, it is natural for every earnest Christian to be concerned about the pathetic condition in which today's church of Jesus Christ is struggling to extricate herself from her current state of spiritual paralysis.

On my accord, I am wondering why the Holy Spirit, centuries ago, decided to entrust me with the burden of leading a New Pentecost under his guidance to liberate the church from its present woes. The only reason I can think of is that just as Jesus chose Paul to lead the early church onto a strong footing by preparing him with His special counseling in the Arabian desert, lavishing on him His inexhaustible grace that He gave to none other than Paul and not even to anyone among His twelve handpicked apostles. He chose me also for no other reason than His decision to lavish me with a lot of grace, which He made available to me more than anyone else in this day and age. In His infinite mercy, He even showed me enough grace to teach me the four-step process of how one can become a born-again Christian, which is something that He didn't show to anyone else—not even Paul! This for no reason other than the immeasurable mercy that He chose to lavish on me for no merit at all on my part!

The Holy Spirit must have anticipated before the foundation of the world what was going to be the condition of Christ's church on this day and at this hour! Therefore, He has put this burden in my heart—the burden of reinstating the basic practice that existed in the early church when the apostles were in charge. The centerpiece of Christian evangelization at that time was to ask the two questions: (1) "Have you received the Holy Spirit?" (Acts 19:2) and (2) "Are you in the faith?" (2 Cor. 13:5). If the answer to any of these two questions was no, there was a follow-up action which the preacher must take. When I say preacher, here I am including every Christian who claimed to be a disciple. In Matthew 28:19–20 when Jesus said, "Therefore go and make disciples of all nations, baptizing them in the name of the Father and of the Son and of the Holy Spirit, and teaching them to obey everything I have commanded you," this duty was assigned to each and every Christian in every nation until everyone in every nation became a disciple. And a disciple meant someone who is undergoing training until he/she becomes like Christ. In Luke 6:40 Jesus says, "A student is not above his master, but everyone who is fully trained would become like his teacher."

As I pointed out above, making sure that a Christian has received the Holy Spirit was the first thing that a disciple who was trying to make someone else a disciple like himself should do. In this regard, I cannot overemphasize the importance of teaching the four-step process of becoming a born-again Christian as is described in the second part of this book.

Furthermore, more than twenty years ago, the Holy Spirit, who knows the need of this hour, chose me to be a prophet and gave me the title The Prophet from Oklahoma City, USA to scream into the ears of the members of an almost dying church like the church in Sardis (Rev. 3:1–6). So my mission is clear: ask each and every fellow Christian that I come across the most important question each and every Christian should be asking no matter which church denomination I go to or what position the believer I am asking occupies in the church denomination he/she belongs to. So here I am to announce to you what is music to my ears as well as to yours.

Dear brothers and sisters in Christ, it is Pentecost time NOW. Slowly but surely, it is time for the final round of the descent of the Holy Spirit prophesied by Peter during that first Pentecost when he spoke to the crowds in Jerusalem quoting prophet Joel in Acts 2:17–21:

> In the last days, God says, I will pour out my Spirit on all people.
>
> Your sons and daughters will prophesy, our young men will see visions, your old men will dream dreams.
>
> Even on my servants, both men and women, I will pour out my Spirit in those days, and they will prophesy.
>
> I will show wonders in the heaven above and signs on the earth below, blood and fire and bellows of smoke.
>
> The sun will be turned to darkness and the moon to blood before the coming of the great and glorious day of the Lord.
>
> And everyone who calls on the name of the Lord will be saved.

A Second Pentecost Is the Greatest Blessing the Church Can Have

There are a few characteristics that make this second Pentecost uniquely different and extra special. First it is the massive scale on which the Holy Spirit is going to be showered on the masses unlike any other time before in the history of the church. It is going to be so widespread in the world that there are two great awakenings that accompany this Pentecost. One is among the preachers who will go around earnestly preaching the Word of God from one end of the globe to the other. The second unique characteristic is that as we read in the prophecy of Joel, the manifestation of the Holy Spirit will take place massively on all people around the world in a gigantic movement the likeness of which has never been seen before. The manifestation will also be gigantic in effectiveness, so much so that huge numbers of believers will call upon the name of the Lord and numerous members of humanity will repent and receive the Holy Spirit. To use an analogy from the American context, let us consider the price of chocolates on and the days leading up to Valentine's Day, which we celebrate on February 14 every year. The price of chocolate candies and chocolate bars will be very high. But immediately after Valentine's Day—on February 15 and the days following—chocolates will be on sale and we can buy chocolate candies and chocolate bars at less than half of the price for the same thing on Valentine's Day. The days of Pentecost following the New Pentecost after the publication of this book will be characterized by a similar manifestation of the Holy Spirit. God's grace showered on those who call on the Name of the Lord during the days of the New Pentecost and during the days after the New Pentecost following the publication of this prophetic book will be massive. It is going to be as though the grace of God that is going to be showered on humanity who call on the name of the Lord will be characterized by the abundance of God's grace witnessed as never before in the history of mankind. Yes, it will be; you can compare it to the price of chocolate after Valentine's Day in the United States on February 15 and during the entire week following February 14! So make sure that you make maximum use of the grace that is going to be abundantly available by the special grace of God during these days!

A third characteristic that will make this final outpouring of the Holy Spirit's indwelling upon the people of God will be a thirst on the part of large numbers of people who will be thirsty for the Word of God as prophesied by another prophet in Amos 8:11, but the true Word of God will be hard to be discerned. Here we read:

> "The days are coming," declares the Sovereign Lord, "when I will send a famine through the land—not a famine of food or a thirst for water, but a famine of hearing the Word of the Lord.
>
> Men will stagger from sea to sea and wander from north to east, searching for the Word of the Lord, but they will not find it.

Well, we are finding many preachers, but the most important message of the gospel is seldom being preached: the need to believe in the Lord Jesus and His gospel with unwavering faith and to repent of our sins as a precondition to be born again as Jesus told Nicodemus in John 3:3. It is time for us as the church of Jesus Christ to bear witness to Him as He has ordered us to do in John 15:27. Therefore, it is time for us to get on our mission to "make disciples of all nations" by undertaking the responsibility to counsel all around us who are not born again to tell them about Jesus and His gospel. It is time for us to be like Paul who boldly and without hindrance preached the kingdom of God and taught about the Lord Jesus Christ.

In 1 Corinthians 4:15–17, Paul writes:

> Even though you have ten thousand guardians in Christ, you do not have many fathers, for in Christ Jesus I became your father through the gospel. Therefore, I urge you to imitate me. For this reason, I am sending to you Timothy, my son whom I love, who is faithful in the Lord. He will remind you of my way of life in Christ Jesus, which agrees with what I teach everywhere in every church.

It is important that we sit down one-on-one with others and share the gospel in its essence to explain to others how our personal life match with what we preach. We should reach out to others as Timothy did and present and share the gospel not only in word but also in deed by becoming a model for them. Those who listen to us must see it in our own actions when we tell them how we can be true disciples of Jesus by "coming to Jesus hating one's father and mother, one's wife and children, one's brothers and sisters—yes, even one's own life." Thus, like Paul and Timothy, we also should show them how we can become not just one of their many guardians in Christ by sharing the gospel, but rather become "their spiritual father" by helping them to become born-again Christians. This calls for dedicated devotion to coach others in the Word of God not only in word but in action as well. So let me share the four steps that a Christian should take to be born again.

The first step is to read and believe in the Word of God in a logical order so as to induce divine life into the soul of the Christian who is trying to recapture the divine life, which he lost by the sin of Adam, the first man. This is done by inviting the Holy Spirit to take residence in that soul by receiving and believing in the name of Jesus (John 1:12) just as God breathed life into the nostrils of Adam after God formed him from the dust of the ground (Gen. 2:7). But the order in which he should read/hear the Word of God and believe is to be chosen carefully so that the Holy Spirit can first induce life into the soul of the believer through his faith in the Word of God when he believes.

Therefore, the reading/hearing of the Word of God has to be done in such a way that first it makes him come spiritually alive. It is for this reason that the following method should be followed as closely as possible. The reading/hearing of the Word of God should be done in this order so that a Christian can first become spiritually alive in Christ according to John 1:12 and then his life in Christ can grow deeper through a deeper knowledge of Christ. The logical order for reading the following selected passages in the Bible is very important as follows:

1. John 1–3
2. Romans 1–6
3. Hebrews 1–6
4. Ephesians 1–5
5. Philippians 1–4
6. Colossians 1–3
7. 1 Timothy 1
8. 1 Peter 1–2
9. 2 Peter 1
10. 1 John 1–5

The second step is to read several times the above scriptural passages in that order and study them and make them familiar to your memory as well as part of your everyday life. In this case, it is to be pointed out that as we read the above passages from the various books of the Bible as outlined in step 1 above, the Holy Spirit will first make a spiritually dead Christian become spiritually alive. The reason why this will happen is found in Hebrews 4:7 and Hebrews 4:12. In Hebrews 4:7 we read, "Today, if you hear his voice, do not harden our hearts." In Hebrews 4:12 we read, "For the word of God is living and active. Sharper than any double-edged sword, it penetrates even to dividing soul and spirit, joints and marrow; it judges the thoughts and attitudes of the heart."

As a Christian reads the various passages outlined above, first his spirit comes alive. Then the Holy Spirit who comes to take residence in him uses the Word of God, which is compared to a double-edged sword, to cut off what is sinful and against the will of God in the believer's life including his soul, mind, and body. The Spirit also plants whatever is lacking in him such as the fruit of the Spirit—love, joy, peace, patience, kindness, goodness, faithfulness, gentleness, and self-control (Gal. 5:22). Thus, he becomes more and more like Christ as each day passes after he has begun his spiritual transformation.

Thus, a Christian, as he is being transformed into the image of Christ in the spiritual sense, will be producing the fruit of the Spirit as we read above. You may have noticed and wondered why it says *fruit* and not *fruits*. The reason is that all these nine "fruits" are like the petals in a rose flower. Just as we don't call a rose flower *roses* because there are nine petals in that flower, the Holy Spirit does not call the nine "fruits" of the Holy Spirit listed in Galatians 5:22 as nine fruits. Another reason is that in a born-again Christian, the Holy Spirit always produces all the nine "fruits" listed in Galatians 5:22 in unison. In other words, either it is all of them coexisting in a believer or it is none of them found. In other words, the "fruits" of the Holy Spirit cannot exist in isolation, meaning only one or two "fruits" only.

This is extremely important for another reason also. When a believer becomes a born-again Christian, he is transformed by producing all the "fruits" of the Holy Spirit and not just only one or two out of the nine. By this token, the transformation brings about changes within the all-around spiritual essence of such a Christian. Thus, his total perspective on life changes. His way of thinking, his priorities, his longings, his interests, his goals in life, his all-around behavior, etc. are all changed. He may not have been in the habit of reading the Word of God on a daily basis, but now that he is transformed, he will not only read the Word of God more frequently but also what he reads in the Word of God will likely be his meditations and the subject of his conversation when he is conversing with others, etc. In other words, the transformation will be total and all-encompassing, including his interactions with others, etc.

In his case, the transformation will be so profound that it will be true of him that even though he lives on this earth, his thoughts and aspirations will be centered on heavenly matters. Thus, what we read in Colossians 3:1–3 will always be literally true in his case. Thus, chances are that his heart and mind will always be set on heavenly things and not on earthly things. In a nutshell, as we read in verse 3, "His life will now be hidden with Christ in God."

The third step is that the Holy Spirit disciplines the Christian being born again through this four-step process in such a way that he learns to obey the Word of God more and more. Each second of the day the Holy Spirit will keep reminding him of what we read in Hebrews 4:7: "Today, if you hear his voice, do not harden your hearts." Thus, before long, the Christian being born again through this process learns to obey the Word of God increasingly more and more and disobey God less and less. Gradually, he gets to a level of obedience when he will be totally controlled by the Word of God just as an alcoholic comes to be controlled by the alcohol which he increasingly consumes as each day passes by. Soon, as we read in Romans 8:14, he becomes increasingly controlled by the Spirit of God so as to be led by the Spirit.

At this point, we can safely say that he has become a born-again Christian because according to Romans 8:14, "Those who are led by the Spirit of God are sons of God." He is now fast approaching the point where it may be very hard or even impossible to commit any serious sin as we read in 1 John 3:9. Here we read, "No one who is born of God will continue to sin, because God's seed remains in him; he cannot go on sinning, because he has been born of God." Another phenomenon that takes place within a Christian who undergoes spiritual transformation through this third step is that he will go through many sufferings as well. This is so because as we read in Hebrew 5:8 that although He was a Son (of the Father), Jesus Christ Himself learned obedience from sufferings and thus became a source of salvation for those who obey Him by suffering also.

The fourth and final step of the rebirth of a Christian to become a born-again Christian is found in Ephesians 3:16–19, which is a prayer of Paul for the church in Ephesus. Here we read:

> "I pray that out of his glorious riches he may strengthen you with power through his Spirit in your inner being, so that Christ may dwell in your hearts through faith. And I pray that you, being rooted and established in love, may have power, together with all the saints, to grasp how wide and long and high and deep is the love of Christ, and to know this love that surpasses knowledge— that you may be filled to the measure of all the fullness of God."

An important thing to note here is that at this point, the Christian who has been born again comes to find out the various dimensions of Christ's love to such an extent that he becomes like another Paul or Peter! Such a born-again Christian comes to find out that Christ's love is so wide that it is as wide as the east is from the west (Ps. 103:12)! It is so long that it is as far as how far God throws our sins behind Him as we read elsewhere. It is so deep that it is as deep as how deep God hurls our sins into the depths of the deepest sea (Mic. 7:19)! In other words, Christ's love for us surpasses our knowledge in all dimensions that we can think of in all kinds of different ways (Eph. 3:18)

An Infinite Capacity to Love Is the Hallmark of Being Born Again

Look at God's infinite love which knows no boundaries; it is so great, wide, long, and deep that it exceeds the farthest extents of every type of dimension that we can think of or imagine. Therefore, I tried to break it down to a more practical level like that of a panoramic structure that will, spiritually speaking, enable us to throw our arms around God's love as well as comprehend it at an intellectually manageable level. I have come to the conclusion that it can be compared to a list of various Christian virtues that we commonly can practice in our everyday living stretched beyond the maximum ability humanly possible. Thus, I came across the following extraordinary expressions of human goodness displayed by Mother Teresa in her life. I would like to share them here for your consideration and edification. It goes something like this under the title do it anyway:

> People are often unreasonable and self-centered – Forgive Them Anyway!
>
> If you are kind, people may accuse you of ulterior motives – Be Kind Anyway!
>
> If you are successful, you will win some false friends and some true enemies – Succeed Anyway!
>
> What you spend years building someone can destroy overnight – Build Anyway!
>
> If you are honest, people may cheat you – Be Honest Anyway!

If you find happiness, people may be jealous –
Be Happy Anyway!

The good you do today may be forgotten tomorrow – Do Good Anyway!

Give the world the best you have and it may
never be enough – Give Your Best Anyway!

For you see, in the end, it is between you and
God – It was never between you and them anyway! (Mother Teresa of Calcutta)

There is an admonition to pursue this kind of absolutely perfect love that we see St. Paul talk about in Ephesians 3:19 that we
saw above. What Mother Teresa refers to above is nothing short of
practicing this kind of perfect godly love because in all of the above
action verbs that Mother Teresa is advocating, there is a negative and
disappointing result that is being anticipated by her. But Mother Teresa is nevertheless advocating to pursue all of the above commands
in spite of all the negative anticipations she had because that is what
a love that surpasses knowledge should look like in our practical
Christian life.

In summary, this was the type of love also that Jesus exhibited on
the cross even though He was very well aware of the fact that the vast
majority of the people that He died for will reject His infinite love on
the cross, but He still demonstrated such a perfect love never before
demonstrated by anyone else.

This is the highest form of love that a Christian can demonstrate
toward his fellow brothers and sisters. That is why the Word of God
here points out this kind of love that "surpasses knowledge" as the
final goal for every born-again Christian to aim for in his spiritual
life. This kind of *agape* love in this perfect form can only be seen on
the cross demonstrated by Jesus! And the calling of every Christian is
to acquire and demonstrate this kind of perfect agape love in his daily
Christian living.

Paul encourages every Christian to acquire and master this kind of pure Christian love in his daily life when he prays for the Colossian church in his lofty prayer in Colossians 1:10–14. Here we read:

> And we pray this in order that you may live a life worthy of the Lord and may please him in every way: bearing fruit in every good work, growing in the knowledge of God, being strengthened with all power according to his glorious might so that you may have great endurance and patience, and joyfully giving thanks to the Father, who has qualified you to share in the inheritance of the saints in the kingdom of light. For he has rescued us from the dominion of darkness and brought us into the kingdom of the Son he loves, in whom we have redemption, the forgiveness of sins.

As a result of such a transformation, we saw above that there are many fruits of the Spirit that a born-again Christian comes to enjoy, one of which is very important—peace. This peace, not only like all other fruits of the Spirit listed in Galatians 5:22, transcends all understanding but also guards the hearts and minds of all the born-again Christians as we read in Philippians 4:7. Thus, their hearts and minds will also be totally transformed to conform to the heart and mind of Christ who is seated at the right hand of the Father as we read in Colossians 3:1. Such a state of mind and heart is characteristic of Christ Himself, and that is why when we are born again, we can confidently say that our life is hidden in Christ and therefore we can enjoy His peace also! Peter also prays for the spiritual perfection of the church in 2 Peter 1:5–8.

How Can a Born-Again Christian Grow in Holiness and Godliness?

a)   By training himself to be more godly

We read in Hebrews 2:1–4:

> We must pay more careful attention, therefore, to what we have heard, so that we do not drift away. For if the message spoken by angels was binding, and every violation and disobedience received its just punishment, how shall we escape if we ignore such a great salvation? This salvation, which was first announced by the Lord, was confirmed to us by those who heard him. God also testified to it by signs, wonders and various miracles, and gifts of the Holy Spirit, distributed according to His will.

Even after one is born again, such a Christian has to ensure that he does not drift away from the new life he has entered into by paying attention to what the Word of God says with regard to how we should live. For example, in 1 Timothy 4:7–8, Paul tells Timothy, "Have nothing to do with godless myths and old wives' tales; rather train yourself to be godly. For physical training is of some value, but godliness has value for all things, holding promise for both the present life and the life to come." Yes, on a daily basis, a born-again Christian has to train himself to be more and more godly so that he can become more and more like Jesus as he is waiting and preparing to meet Him after completing his journey on this planet.

This he does by using his Spirit-given spiritual gifts. Thus, Paul tells Timothy in 1 Timothy 4:13–14, "Until I come, devote yourself to the public reading of Scripture, to preaching and to teaching. Do not neglect your gift, which was given to you through a prophetic message when the body of elders laid their hands on you." Thus, a born-again Christian also must try to devote himself to serving others and thus becoming more and more godly using the gifts of the Holy Spirit which he received when he was born again. This will ensure that he makes good progress on his spiritual journey which he started when he was "born of the Spirit" as he was born again!

b) *By training himself to rejoice in his sufferings*

In Romans 5:3–5 we read, "We also rejoice in our sufferings, because we know that suffering produces perseverance; perseverance, character; and character, hope. And hope does not disappoint us, because God has poured out his love into our hearts by the Holy Spirit, whom he has given us." When we live as born-again Christians, according to the Word of God, we will have to go through many sufferings. But in the middle of the suffering that we go through, the Holy Spirit who has taken residence within us will help us to rejoice even while we are suffering as joy is one of the fruits that the Holy Spirit produces in us. This joy is created within us through the power of the Holy Spirit by giving us the patience to endure these sufferings. For example, it will give us the patience to count from one to twenty or as needed, without reacting to the pain caused by the sufferings we are experiencing.

This kind of ability that the Holy Spirit gives us is called perseverance. When a born-again Christian goes through this kind of patience-building exercise, he gradually develops a character that is pleasing to God, which will create the ability within him to hope for the glory to come after his life on this earth. This hope will give him the ability to withstand all and every suffering he experiences by the grace of God. Such an ability will give endurance for such a Christian to go through all kinds of sufferings he will be experiencing in his life.

In Hebrews 10:19–25, we read:

> Therefore, brothers, since we have confidence to enter the Most Holy Place by the blood of Jesus, by a new and living way opened for us through the curtain, that is, his body, and since we have a great priest over the house of God, let us draw near to God with a sincere heart in full assurance of faith, having our hearts sprinkled to cleanse us from a guilty conscience and having our bodies washed with pure water. Let us hold unswervingly to the hope we profess, for he who promised is faithful. And let us consider how we may spur one another on toward love and good deeds. Let us not give up meeting together, as some are in the habit of doing, but let us encourage one another—and all the more as you see the Day approaching.

In the Bible, we see how three heroes, namely Paul, Joseph, and Job, unswervingly held on to their faith by persevering in their troubles and the difficulties they faced. These three all had unshakable faith in God which they built up through difficult experiences and extremely trying circumstances. We also are encouraged to do the same when life's trials test us almost beyond what we think we can handle. This is the lesson that the author of Hebrews is teaching us through the above passage.

But having built up such a strong faith and trust in God who has promised us that He will carry us through whatever circumstances and trials that He may put us through, we must then try to help our brothers and sisters to get to the same level of faith and trust in God, which we have built up for ourselves. Thus, we should gather souls for eternity for the greater love of God by resorting to a life of evangelization and merciful acts of kindness. In carrying this mission that God desires for each of our lives, there is no boundary, so much so that we should be prepared to sacrifice our own lives for the sake of Christ just as He has done for us. When we do this, as we read in James 1:12, what is promised to those who sincerely and deeply love God will easily be within our reach. Also, by doing this, we will certainly receive from God the crown of life to enjoy the eternal bliss that God has promised to everyone who loves God as we read in James 1:12!

How Can We Perfect Our New Life in the Spirit after Being Born Again?

In Galatians 5:22, we read that one of the fruits of the Holy Spirit is meekness, which is defined as the power under control given by the Holy Spirit to act with the same kind of calmness and gentleness that Jesus displayed when He was scourged, crowned with thorns, and horribly treated by the Roman soldiers as He was suffering beyond imagination to redeem the world by making atonement for humanity's sins. We also are called to display this same kind of meekness if we want to truly become a born-again Christian.

That is why in Galatians 6:1 we are commanded to "restore someone who is caught in a sin" if we are or want to be truly spiritual. But the apostle Paul warns us here that we should "watch ourselves" so that we also may not be "tempted" to lose our own temperament and fall into the same sin committed by those whom we are trying to restore. Then again in Ephesians 4:1–3, the apostle urges us "to live a life worthy of the calling we have received by being completely humble and gentle; being patient, bearing with one another in love and thus to make every effort to keep the unity of the Spirit through the bond of peace."

To do the above is not easy. To illustrate the point, Apostle Paul points out how he himself acted while he was in this sort of situation in his own spiritual life. Thus, in 1 Thessalonians 2:7–13 he says:

> As apostles of Christ we could have been a burden to you, but we were gentle among you, like a mother caring for her little children. We loved you so much that we were delighted to share with

you not only the gospel of God but our lives as well, because you had become so dear to us. Surely you remember, brothers, our toil and hardship; we worked night and day in order not to be a burden to anyone while we preached the gospel of God to you.

You are witnesses, and so is God, of how holy, righteous and blameless we were among you who believed. For you know how we dealt with each of you as a father deals with his own children, encouraging, comforting and urging you to live lives worthy of God, who calls you into his kingdom and glory. And we also thank God continually because, when you received the Word of God, which you heard from us, you accepted it not as the word of men, but as it actually is, the word of God, which is at work in you who believe.

When we live like this among others in this sinful world, there is surely a reward that God promises us as we read in Isaiah 40:10–11: "See, the Sovereign Lord comes with power, and his arm rules for him. See, his reward is with him, and his recompense accompanies him. He tends his flock like a shepherd: He gathers the lambs in his arms and carries them close to his heart; he gently leads those that have young."

Thus, when we live like Paul, carrying one another's burdens and setting an example for others, Jesus will reward us for what we do even though we may have to go through many sufferings in the process of doing it. That is what God tells us through the words of Isaiah in the above passage (Isa. 40:10–11). And thus, we are challenged by the apostle Paul to conduct ourselves in our new life as a born-again Christian!

In Hebrews 10:38–39 we read:

> So do not throw away your confidence, it will be richly rewarded. You need to persevere so that when you have done the will of God, you will receive what has been promised. For in just a very little while, He who is coming will come and will not delay. But my righteous one will live by faith. And if he shrinks back, I will not be pleased with him. But we are not of those who shrink back and are destroyed, but of those who believe and are saved.

In this passage, once a Christian has been born again and continues on his spiritual journey, he is once again warned against discouragement that will certainly come later on when things get tough while sticking to our faith and trying to persevere. Sometimes our faith may be faced with doubts brought by Satan for derailing us from our path of perseverance. The author of Hebrews is telling us in Hebrews 10:37–38 that we should not "shrink back" when we face these doubts and thoughts of discouragement. The way we overcome these negative thoughts of doubts and discouragement is by holding on to our faith with the help of God and the power of the Holy Spirit. We do this also by often reminding ourselves that there is great reward for all the hard work we do working for the glory of God and for "doing good, for at the proper time we will reap a harvest if we do not give up." Therefore, as we have opportunity, let us do good to all people, especially to those who belong to the family of believers as we read in Galatians 6:9–10.

Also, when we are born again, we receive the Spirit of sonship by whom we cry out, "Abba, Father" even as "the Spirit Himself testifies with our spirit that we are God's children. Now if we are children, then we are heirs—heirs of God and coheirs with Christ, if indeed we share in his sufferings in order that we may also share in his glory." To what extent do we become coheirs with Christ and share in His glory? It is almost impossible to think of the glory we are going to share with Christ! Because in Revelations 3:21–22, it says, "to him who overcomes, He will give the right to sit with Him on His throne, just as He overcame and sat down with His Father on His throne." In other words, as we read in 2 Timothy 2:12: "If we endure, we will also reign with Him."

This kind of ability, which the Holy Spirit gives us, is called perseverance. When a born-again Christian goes through this kind of patience-building exercise, he gradually develops a character that is pleasing to God, which will create the ability within such a Christian to hope for the glory to come after his life on this earth is over. This hope will give him the ability to withstand all and every suffering he experiences by the grace of God. Such an ability will give endurance for the Christian to go through all kinds of sufferings he will be experiencing in his life while experiencing joy all the time. This is how a Christian can overcome all kinds of sufferings in his new life as a born-again Christian!

Most of us have been taught that the rebirth of a Christian is brought about by baptism whether it is received as a child or as an adult. But if we study the Scriptures, we find that the rebirth of a Christian is brought about by an act of God based on a choice made by God Himself even before the foundation of this world. This we find in Ephesians 1:4–5 where we read, "He [God] chose us in him before the creation of the world to be holy and blameless in his sight. In love He predestined us to be adopted as his sons through Jesus Christ, in accordance with His pleasure and will…" We find this also in 2 Timothy 1:9 where we read, "God has saved us and called us to a holy life—not because of anything we have done but because of his own purpose and grace. This grace was given us in Christ Jesus before the beginning of time."

This action of choosing and electing is the fulfillment of an Old Testament prophecy that God made through Prophet Ezekiel stated in Ezekiel 36:25–27 where we read:

> "I will sprinkle clean water on you, and you
> will be clean; I will cleanse you from all your im-
> purities and from all your idols. I will give you a
> new heart and put a new spirit in you; I will re-
> move from you your heart of stone and give you a
> heart of flesh. And I will put my Spirit in you and
> move you to follow my decrees and be careful to
> keep my laws."

So, the rebirth of a man is strictly the work of God and God only. However, on the part of the one being baptized, his contribution is his faith in God. That is why Jesus says in John 15:5, "I am the vine; you are the branches. If a man remains in me and in him, he will bear much fruit; apart from me you can do nothing."

Thus, as described above, the rebirth of a Christian as a child of God is a God-initiated and God-completed process. Therefore, St. Paul is admonishing us to "continue to work out our salvation with fear and trembling because it is God who works in us to will and to act according to his good purpose." Now we may ask, "How does God initiate and complete the rebirth of a Christian?" We saw above how God chooses an individual in Christ to be a child of God before the beginning of time (Eph. 1:4).

To illustrate this process, let us imagine a picture of a Christian being placed in a book. Just as the picture travels to wherever the book is carried around, a child chosen in Christ goes wherever Christ goes and experiences whatever Christ experiences. Thus, when Christ died on the cross physically, all Christians chosen by God in Christ also died. And when Christ rose from death on the third day, every Christian chosen by God in Christ also rose with Christ. When a Christian is baptized, he is only externally participating in Christ's death and resurrection just as under the law of Moses the Israelites were circumcised ONLY as an external symbol of their being set apart as the people of God (Josh. 5:7).

Thus, when a Christian has participated in Christ's death and resurrection by the choice of God before the beginning of time and physically this choice is marked by the baptism of such a Christian, there is an invisible transformation that takes place. Just as Abraham's faith is credited to him as imputed righteousness (Gen. 15:6), a baptized Christian also receives imputed righteous ness from God ONLY if he is ALSO chosen in Christ by God before the beginning of time. Again, just as Abraham exhibited great faith in God's promises to him and this faith is credited to him as righteousness, a baptized Christian's faith is credited to him as righteousness.

Consequently, just as Abraham did not hesitate to obey when he was asked to sacrifice his son Isaac, a Christian receives the grace to live a holy and blameless life in Christ ONLY by the grace offered to him by the merits of Jesus's death on the cross. At this point, a baptized Christian becomes a born-again Christian not because of anything he gains from his physical baptism but because of him being born again as a child of God receiving "forgiveness of sins through the blood of Jesus Christ in accordance with the riches of God's grace that God lavishes on him" (Eph. 1:7–8).

> As a result, he becomes a regenerated Christian who no longer offers the parts of his body to sin as instruments of wickedness, but rather offers himself to God as one being brought from death to life, offering the parts of his body to God as instruments of righteousness. From this point on, sin will not be his master, because he is not under law, but under grace. (Rom. 6:13–14)

In this instance, I would like to point out that going for confession, which is the regular way that the Catholics get rid of sins in our past life, is ONLY a temporary relief from sin which is only a Band-Aid solution to a problem that needs a major surgery. It usually ends up in the one who confesses his sins to a priest falling back again to his sinful ways before long. But when one is born again, as we read in 1 John 3:9, "Because God's seed remains in him, he cannot go on sinning, because he has been born of God." Here, the spiritual transformation is permanent—for life—whereas the relief from sin through confession is probably 95 percent of the time only temporary! Because in this case, the remission from sin is not lasting as in the case of the spiritual transformation that takes place when a Christian is born again, which is a total transformation in the spiritual genetic composition of a Christian. That is why he cannot sin again as we read in 1 John 3:9.

A Born-Again Christian Will be Taught by the Spirit to Live Without Sin!

Some facts we should know about this claim from the Word of God:

1. After all, according to Ephesians 1:4, the very purpose why God created us was for us "to be holy and blameless in His sight." This is what we achieve when we live as born-again Christians which is what God expects of us.

2. But "holy and blameless in His sight" does not mean *sinless*, which none of us can be according to 1 John 1:8. Here we read, "If we claim to be without sin, we deceive ourselves and the truth is not in us." So here the Word of God is telling us that we cannot be sinless! How do we reconcile the two? The answer is found in the next paragraph, in the point I'm going to explain below.

3. We cannot be sinless, but we can be "holy and blameless in His sight." How can this be possible? The answer is found in Psalm 19:13 where we read, "Keep your servant also from willful sins; may they not rule over me. Then will I be blameless, innocent of great transgression." So the key here is to live a "holy and blameless" life. When we do this, we can become sinless also by doing what the Word of God tells us to do in 1 John 1:9. Here we read, "If we confess our sins [sins that are mortal sins which are referred to as "willful sins" in Ps. 19:13], He is faithful and just and will forgive us of such sins and purify us from all unrighteousness."

So, we do not need to go for confessions for sins that are not *mortal sins* if we are Catholics. For those who are non-Catholics, confessing our sins is not an option; in that case, confessing our sins to God directly after repenting of our sins would suffice for not being able to confess to a priest. Such sins (*mortal sins*) are referred to as "willful sins" in Psalm 19:13. But after becoming a born-again Christian and growing in godliness and holiness as we have seen above, even the very root of our thoughts and the thought process will be made as holy as God's own thoughts and thought process as we read in 1 Peter 1:16 which says, "Be holy, because I am holy." If becoming as holy as God is not possible, God would not have asked us to be "as holy as God." This is also probably why the Word of God says that if we are born again, we can live without sin as we read in 1 John 3:9.

To recap what we are saying here, for those who are Catholics, they can either repent of their willful sins and confess them to a priest or simply repent of their sins and then confess them directly to God; and then according to 1 John 1:9, all their unrighteousness will be completely wiped out by God. But for a born-again Christian, since he cannot sin according to 1 John 5:18, he may still commit sins that are not willful. For example, for any white lies he may say to do a charitable deed, all that he needs to do is to confess to God directly, and the unintended sin (which he committed like a white lie) will be wiped out by God. For those of you who want a definition of a white lie, a good example will be this. Suppose one of my friends comes to visit me unexpectedly during lunchtime. I have food only for myself. Then if I offer the food that I have to him, he may not eat if I tell him I haven't eaten. But if I say I already ate my lunch before he came (which is a white lie), then my friend will probably eat, and this is the only way I can persuade him to eat. In this case, the purpose behind my telling a lie is only to do an act of charity; and therefore, my telling the lie is not a willful sin. In this case, just tell God, or you may not even have to confess it since He already knows, that your lie was to do something good to help your friend! So, this kind of white lie or any other similar act of kindness, which is intended for doing something good, is not a willful sin that you do not even have to confess. But it doesn't hurt to confess it to God. Either way, this is not counted by God as a sin. But a born-again Christian can commit only this kind of sin; and in this case, whether he confesses it or not, he will be sinless. I thought I will make it clear for those who did not have a clear idea on this subject.

Some Foundational Guidelines to Optimize Our Spiritual Journey Based on the Word of God

In life, we can build only on the foundation already laid by Christ as we read in 1 Corinthians 3:11–15. However, we have the choice to build on this foundation "using gold, silver, costly stones, wood, hay or straw" as we further read here. Paul continues to elaborate on this point in 1 Corinthians 3:13–15 and says:

> "Our work will be shown for what it is, because the Day will bring it to light. It will be revealed with fire, and the fire will test the quality of each man's work. If what he has built survives, he will receive his reward. If it is burned up, he will suffer loss; he himself will be saved, but only as one escaping through the flames."

We can build with gold on the foundation of Christ by living according to two other principles: the Philippians 4:4–7 principle and the Philippians 4:8–9 principle. The Philippians 4:4–7 principle states:

> "Rejoice in the Lord always. I will say it again: Rejoice! Let your gentleness be evident to all. The Lord is near. Do not be anxious about anything, but in everything, by prayer

and petition, with thanksgiving, present your requests to God. And the peace of God, which transcends all understanding, will guard your hearts and your minds in Christ Jesus."

The Philippians 4:8–9 principle states:

"Finally, brothers, whatever is true, whatever is noble, whatever is right, whatever is pure, whatever is lovely, whatever is admirable— if anything is excellent or praiseworthy— think about such things. Whatever you have learned or received or heard from me, or seen in me— put it into practice. And the God of peace will be with you."

Notice here that we are to aim thinking of doing everything we do in the best way possible whether it be our thoughts, our words, or our deeds. We should do even the simple things we do with the greatest love for God and our neighbor.

Given the above guidelines to do what we do every moment of our lives, we can exercise different levels of diligence, varying degrees of love for God and neighbor, and different levels of spiritual fervor. Thus, we have the following four life models to choose from to make our spiritual life suit our varying spiritual identities, which will vary from individual to individual even though we may all be born-again Christians.

As you may have guessed, in each of these cases, becoming a born-again Christian is a common denominator, and therefore, imitating Christ's life is the centerpiece of each of these spiritual lifestyles. Given this fact, there is some flexibility in choosing one of these four spiritual models for living the kind of Spirit-filled and Spirit-controlled life without losing the identity of a disciple of Christ, who is supposed to be another Christ, as he or she lives in this dark and seemingly lost world as "the salt of the earth and the light of the world." In other words, as we read in Luke 6:40, Jesus says that "a student is not above his teacher, but everyone who is fully trained will be like his teacher."

Thus, the commonality that makes each of us look like Jesus, our Lord and Master, is that as we read in John 1:12, we will all be "children of God—children not born of natural descent, nor of human decision or a husband's will, but born of God," which will give us pretty much the same essence as that of Jesus Himself but with (for lack of a better term) a very slight infinitesimal difference between one another.

Having said that, let us examine the four life models that we can choose from, modeled after Jesus, our Lord and Master, and St. Paul the Apostle, who we can say was pretty much filled with the Word of God and therefore like God Himself (according to what Jesus said in John 10:34–35). The third and fourth spiritual life models are Daniel who is addressed as "most beloved" by God in the book of Daniel (Dan. 10:18) and Jacob, who was named by God as a prince (Gen. 32:28).

I have to make something clear here with regard to Daniel and Jacob which is the fact that these two most beloved individuals belong to the Old Testament and thus before the first Pentecost when the church was born. And as a result, they are according to Jesus's comparison of John the Baptist in Luke 7:28 to someone smaller than the least in the kingdom of God, inferior to Jesus and Paul. Let me leave it at that since I do not have a satisfactory explanation for putting them on par with Jesus and Paul because God called Daniel "most beloved" (Dan. 10:18) and God called Jacob a prince in Genesis 32:28.

We can use one of these life models to gauge how well we measure up against the life model we have selected. Thus, we can evaluate our spiritual life as we go on with our life journey trying to become perfect "as our heavenly Father is perfect," which is our calling according to Jesus (Matt. 5:48). We have to bear in mind that the way we are trying to accomplish this is by "fixing our eyes on Jesus, the author and perfecter of our faith, who for the joy set before him endured the cross, scorning its shame, and sat down at the right hand of the throne of God" as we read in Hebrews 12:2.

The Word of God continues to describe how our attitude in this regard should be in Hebrews 12:3–17 where we read as follows:

> Consider him who endured such opposition from sinful men so that you will not grow weary and lose heart. In your struggle against sin, you have not yet resisted to the point of shedding your blood. And you have forgotten that word of encouragement that addresses you as sons:

> My son, do not make light of the Lord's discipline, and do not lose heart when he rebukes you, because the Lord disciplines those he loves, and he punishes everyone he accepts as a son.

> Endure hardship as discipline; God is treating you as sons. For what son is not disciplined by his father? If you are not disciplined (and everyone undergoes discipline), then you are illegitimate children and not true sons. Moreover, we have all had human fathers who disciplined us and we respected them for it. How much more should we submit to the Father of our spirits and live! Our fathers disciplined us for a little while as they thought best; but God disciplines us for our good, that we may share in his holiness. No discipline seems pleasant at the time, but painful. Later on, however, it produces a harvest of righteousness and peace for those who have been trained by it.

> Therefore, strengthen your feeble arms and weak knees. "Make level paths for your feet,"

so that the lame may not be disabled, but rather healed."

Make every effort to live in peace with all men and to be holy; without holiness no one will see the Lord. See to it that no one misses the grace of God and that no bitter root grows up to cause trouble and defile many. See that no one is sexually immoral, or is godless like Esau, who for a single meal sold his inheritance rights as the oldest son. Afterward, as you know, when he wanted to inherit this blessing, he was rejected. He could bring about no change of mind, though he sought the blessing with tears.

A. *We can live our spiritual lives using Christ as our spiritual life model.*

We can be born-again Christians and then try to live imitating Christ and aiming to achieve Jesus's perfection every moment of our life by perfecting our born-again Christian life and growing in godliness and holiness. I have described this under my FOUR SIMPLE STEPS to become a born-again Christian method. When we live our lives using Christ as our model, we will be living pretty much by the Matthew 5:48 principle. In Matthew 5:48, Jesus tells us, "Be ye perfect, just as your heavenly Father is perfect." Again, Jesus tells us in Luke 6:36, "Be ye merciful, just as your Father is merciful." Also, He tells us in John 4:34, "My food is to do the will of Him who sent me and to finish His work."

To attain such perfection, living 24-7, 365 days a year by the 1 Thessalonians 5:16–18 principle will also go a long way. In 1 Thessalonians 5:16–18 we read, "Be joyful always; pray continually; give thanks in all circumstances, for this is God's will for you in Christ Jesus."

(Note: In each of the three life models presented here—namely, that of Paul, Daniel, and Jacob, the first two paragraphs below each title are repeated since becoming a born-again Christian is common to all life profiles presented here whether it is of Paul, Daniel, or Jacob.)

B. We can live our spiritual lives using Paul as our spiritual life model.

For this, we become a born-again Christian and then try to live imitating Paul and aiming to achieve Jesus's perfection pretty much to the same degree as how Christ lived. When we live our lives using Paul as our model, we will be living pretty much by the Matthew 5:48 principle. In Matthew 5:48 Jesus tells us, "Be ye perfect, just as your heavenly Father is perfect." Again, Jesus tells us in Luke 6:36, "Be ye merciful, just as your Father is merciful." Also, He tells us in John 4:34, "My food is to do the will of Him who sent me and to finish His work."

To attain such perfection, living 24-7, 365 days a year by the 1 Thessalonians 5:16–18 principle will also go a long way. In 1 Thessalonians 5:16–18 we read, "Be joyful always; pray continually; give thanks in all circumstances, for this is God's will for you in Christ Jesus."

We can also adopt two other principles that distinguish Paul from all other heroes of faith we see in the history of the church. These two principles that Paul lived by are the Philippians 3:4–11 principle and the Acts 20:22–24 principle. The Philippians 3:4–11 principle says in Paul's own words:

> **If anyone else thinks he has reasons to put confidence in the flesh, I have more: circumcised on the eighth day, of the people of Israel, of the tribe of Benjamin, a Hebrew of Hebrews, in regard to the law, a Pharisee; as for zeal, persecuting the church; as for legalistic**

righteousness, faultless. But whatever was to my profit I now consider a loss for the sake of Christ. What is more, I consider everything a loss compared to the surpassing greatness of knowing Christ Jesus my Lord, for whose sake I have lost all things. I consider them rubbish, that I may gain Christ and be found in him, not having a righteousness of my own that comes from the law, but that which is through faith in Christ—the righteousness that comes from God and is by faith. I want to know Christ and the power of his resurrection and the fellowship of sharing in his sufferings, becoming like him in his death, and so, somehow, to attain to the resurrection from the dead.

The Acts 20:22–24 principle says in Paul's own words:

And now, compelled by the Spirit, I am going to Jerusalem, not knowing what will happen to me there. I only know that in every city the Holy Spirit warns me that prison and hardships are facing me. However, I consider my life worth nothing to me, if only I may finish the race and complete the task the Lord Jesus has given me—the task of testifying to the gospel of God's grace.

C. *We can live our spiritual lives using Daniel as our spiritual life model.*

For this, we become a born-again Christian and then try to live imitating Daniel and aiming to achieve Jesus's perfection to a degree pretty much as perfect as Paul's but maybe one notch below that of Paul. When we live our lives using Daniel as our model, we will be living pretty much by the Matthew 5:48 principle. In Matthew 5:48 Jesus tells us, "Be ye perfect, just as your heavenly Father is perfect." Again, Jesus tells us in Luke 6:36, "Be ye merciful, just as your Father is merciful." Also, He tells us in John 4:34, "My food is to do the will of Him who sent me and to finish His work." To attain such perfection, living 24-7, 365 days a year by the 1 Thessalonians 5:16–18 principle will also go a long way. In 1 Thessalonians 5:16–18 we read, "Be joyful always; pray continually; give thanks in all circumstances, for this is God's will for you

in Christ Jesus."

We can also adopt three other principles that separate Daniel from the other heroes of faith we see in the history of the church. These three principles that Daniel lived by are the Daniel 1:8 principle, the Daniel 6:10 principle, and the Daniel 12:3 principle.

The Daniel 1:8 principle that Daniel always lived by was that "he resolved not to defile himself with the royal food and wine, and he asked the chief official for permission not to defile himself this way." The reason was that he feared that some of that royal food may have been offered to the idol gods that King Nebuchadnezzar worshiped.

Then in Daniel 6:10 we read that Daniel was a man of prayer. This is evident from Daniel 6:10 where we read, "Now when Daniel learned that the decree had been published, he went home to his upstairs room where the windows opened toward Jerusalem. Three times a day he got down on his knees and prayed, giving thanks to his God, just as he had done before." This was a daily habit for Daniel to pray to his God at least three times a day, and he had a special room for it.

And finally, the third Daniel principle was that he worked as hard as he could to bring others to righteousness. This he did about, which we find out from a vision that he had as we see described in Daniel 12:10–13 in which he learned that there was great reward in heaven for those leading others to righteousness. This we read in Daniel 12:3, "Those who are wise will shine like the brightness of the heavens, and those who lead many to righteousness, like the stars for ever and ever."

Even though Daniel was not as blessed as Paul, Daniel was endearing to God so much so that in the book of Daniel, we saw Daniel was twice addressed by Jesus Christ in the visions that he had in which Jesus saluted Daniel by two of the most endearing salutations ("Most Beloved" and "Highly Esteemed") used in the entire Bible one of which was used by God the Father Himself to salute Jesus when He was baptized by John the Baptist (Matthew 3:17). This we saw in Daniel 10:11 and Daniel 10:18. In Daniel 10:18, we read that Jesus gave Daniel strength by touching him to listen to the truths about what will happen at the end of times and at the end of the universe. But above all, God gave him the promise, "At the end of his days, he would receive his allotted inheritance [in heaven]" (Daniel 12:13). He shared this truth with us to encourage us and to boost our spiritual stamina when he wrote in Daniel 12:3:

> Those who are wise will shine like the brightness of the heavens, and those who lead many to righteousness, like the stars forever and ever.

D. We can live our spiritual lives using Jacob as our spiritual life model.

For this, we become a born-again Christian and then try to live imitating Jacob and aiming to achieve Jesus's perfection to a degree pretty much as perfect as Daniel's but maybe one notch below that of Daniel. When we live our lives using Jacob as our model, we will be living pretty much by the Matthew 5:48 principle. In Matthew 5:48 Jesus tells us, "Be ye perfect, just as your heavenly Father is perfect." Again, Jesus tells us in Luke 6:36, "Be ye merciful, just as your Father is merciful." Also, He tells us in John 4:34, "My food is to do the will of Him who sent me and to finish His work."

To attain such perfection, living 24-7, 365 days a year by the 1 Thessalonians 5:16–18 principle will also go a long way. In 1 Thessalonians 5:16–18 we read, "Be joyful always; pray continually; give thanks in all circumstances, for this is God's will for you in Christ Jesus."

When we read Genesis 32:21–30, I feel that this is the one thing that helped Jacob to become a prince of God, a title that Jacob got from God because in the words of God Himself, Jacob proved himself to be an *overcomer*. The context in which he received this title was an encounter that Jacob had with a man whom he recognized as God only toward the end of the wrestling match that he had with him. Thus, he wrestled with this man during the entire duration of a whole night without recognizing that he was God.

When we read Revelation 2:1 through 3:22, we can also see that in order to receive the blessings of heaven at the end of our lives, we all have to prove ourselves to be overcomers without exception. What we read in Genesis 32:22–30 about how Jacob proved himself to be an overcomer in the eyes of God through his persistent determination will convince us also that this kind of heroic act on the part of Jacob overcoming God was also exactly what the Holy Spirit demanded of everyone in all the seven churches of God described in Revelation 2:1 through Revelation 3:22. I truly believe that this is a valuable lesson that we have to learn from one of our ancient fathers of Faith in the person of Jacob—a lesson as important as becoming a born again Christian if we also want to make it to heaven! No wonder Jesus says in Luke 16:16: "The Law and the Prophets were proclaimed until John. Since that time, the good news of the kingdom of God is being preached, and everyone is forcing his way into it."

Acknowledgments and Announcements

Along with the born-again ministry, which is the central theme of this book *A New Pentecost to a Starving World*, another equally important arm of the Jesus Army Ministry is also being kicked off along with the publication of this most valuable book, which, God willing, will likely be the most influential Christian book ever published since the publication of the Bible. What it involves is the starting and operating of a counseling program going to be based in two centers—one being in India at Paingottoor, Muvattupuzha, Kerala, India, and the other base will be in Dallas, Texas, USA. Please wait for more details on how you can get counseling help from the bornagain ministry on how one can be born again spiritually at these two geographical locations. Please contact me at my temporary email address at jesusarmyministries@yahoo.com, which will be set up sometime after January 1, 2023, when prayer rallies throughout USA and India will be conducted at Catholic worship centers or churches.

Announcements and testimonials from born-again Christians who have been born again through the evangelization efforts of the Born-Again Ministry and information about the prayer rallies will be announced in the form of videos published as part of my Jesus Army Ministry Facebook page. I couldn't be happier in my life as well as thankful to the Lord Jesus Christ for making it possible for me to kick off today these two long-awaited ministries (the born-again ministry and the Prayer Rally Ministry) both at this time along with the publication of this book, *A New Pentecost to a Starving World*.

Please pray for me and the many people who have stood with me or are working with me for the success of this ministry along with Rev. Mathew Naikomparambil, founder of the largest retreat center in the world today, namely the Divine Retreat Center in Muringoor,

Chalakudy, Kerala, India, who has been often called the Billy Graham of India; Rev. Jose Vettiyankal, who has been my spiritual mentor for more than twenty years, is also one of the priests of the Divine Retreat Center Team; and last but not the least, the parish priest of the St. Antony's Forane Catholic Church in my hometown, Paingottoor, Muvattupuzha, Kerala, India. He also blessed me and my ministry when I met him in May of 2022 at the St. Antony's Forane Catholic Church at Paingottoor, Kerala.

At this time, I remember my late beloved mother, Mrs. Rosa Varkey, who passed away from COVID-19 in the year 2020 in a nursing home in North Hollywood, California, USA. I can never thank enough my beloved wife, Annie, who has stood by me all these past fifty years of our wonderful marriage even as we are celebrating our fiftieth wedding anniversary this year for all the support that she has given me not only for carrying the lion's share of my workload around the house, especially during the year 2022 when I was working on my book but also for putting up with me all these years. Above all, I thank Almighty God also for my father who passed away when I was only six years old, whom I most lovingly remember at this most crucial and history-making time in my life.

I am thrilled to report the fact that it was through Rev. Jose Vettiyankal that I received the title the "Prophet from Oklahoma City" in Oklahoma City, Oklahoma State, USA, the state north of the state of Texas, USA, where I currently live. It was here where I shared the Word of God for the first time ever in a Catholic church at the invitation of Rev. Jose Vettiyankal in Oklahoma City, USA. I am also deeply indebted to Rev. Rodolfo Garcia of St. Francis of Assisi Catholic Parish in Frisco, Texas, and Rev. Jacob Christy Parambukattil of St. Alphonsa Catholic Church in Coppell, Texas, USA. I have been greatly inspired and influenced by Rev. Pastor Shibu Thomas Hebron Oklahoma, Oklahoma City, USA, and also Rev. Pastor Richard Ellis and their powerful radio ministries.

Thank you all who stood with me all these years and supported me and my Jesus Army Ministry and the Facebook ministry, and also more importantly, those who will be supporting me more importantly by your prayers and also financially to save as many souls for eternity as possible in the coming years by your support for the success of both the Born-again Ministry and the Prayer Rally Ministry, which the Lord will be guiding through my hands in the two locations, one in India and the other in the United States. I am fully conscious of my inadequacy to manage these two ministries on my own. But as we read in 2 Corinthians 4:1, "Since through God's mercy we have these ministries, we do not lose heart," I am totally relying on the Lord's mercy and abundant grace for the success of these two ministries for the greater glory of God.

Before I go, I would also like to acknowledge two other very important people who have been a source of great inspiration for me to start both of these ministries on these two continents on the two opposite sides of the globe: Rev. Bro. Sabu Aruthottiyil and Bro. Sunil Mosa, both of whom have extended their prayers and other forms of help to my above two ministries in the two most important countries, India and my adopted country the United States, where I am settled now. Both Bro. Sabu Aruthottiyil and Bro. Sunil Mosa, along with Rev. Mani belonging to the Tyler Diocese, are currently running the Grace of Heaven Retreat Center in Winnsboro, Texas, USA, and they have also supported me and inspired me greatly.

Once again, thanks to everyone. But I bend my knees in front of God who has blessed me beyond words and beyond any stretch of imagination to become an Ephesians 3:20 Christian for His greater glory even though I am the least worthy of any of these unimaginable blessings! Praise the Lord, hallelujah!

A Tear-off Page on Prayer Rally

THEAMAZING PRAYER RALLY

Did You Know You Can Gain Heaven for
Shouting Out Just Once the *Two Words…**
*(If this is so, certainly salvation is guaranteed for
anyone who attends* **JUST TWO
PRAYER RALLIES!)**
So Much to Gain*…at So Little Cost!*

What do we gain?

We can gain eternal heaven with all its never-ending pleasures and peace and joy that know no limit!

Question: What do we get in heaven when we die and enter into the presence of God?

Answer: In 1 Corinthians 2:9–10, we read: "No eye has seen, no ear has heard, no mind has conceived what God has prepared for those who love him—but God has revealed it to us by his Spirit."

Answer: In Psalm 16:5–6, we read: "Lord, you have assigned me my portion and my cup; The boundary lines have fallen for me in pleasant places; Surely I have a delightful inheritance."

Answer: In Psalm 16:11, we read: "You have made known to me the path of life; you will fill me with joy in your presence, with eternal pleasures at your right hand."

Answer: In 2 Corinthians 4:17–18, we read: "For our light and momentary troubles are achieving for us an eternal glory that far outweighs them all. So we fix our eyes not on what is seen, but on what is unseen. For what is seen is temporary, but what is unseen is eternal."

Answer: In Matthew 13:41–43, we read: "The Son of Man will send out his angels, and they will weed out of his kingdom everything that causes sin and all who do evil. They will throw them into the fiery furnace, where there will be weeping and gnashing of teeth. Then the righteous will shine like the sun in the kingdom of their Father."

Answer: In Matthew 5:11–12, we read (Jesus telling us): "Blessed are you when people insult you, persecute you and falsely say all kinds of evil against you because of me. Rejoice and be glad, because great is your reward in heaven, for in the same way they persecuted the prophets who were before you."

Answer: In 1 Peter 1:3-5 we read: "Praise be to the God and Father of our Lord Jesus Christ! In his great mercy he has given us new birth into a living hope through the resurrection of Jesus Christ from the dead, and into an inheritance that can never perish, spoil or fade… kept in heaven for you, who through faith are shielded by God's power until the coming of the salvation that is ready to be revealed in the last time."

Answer: In John 14:1–2, we read: "Do not let your heart be troubled. Trust in God; trust also in Me. In My Father's house are many mansions; if it were not so, I would have told you. I am going there to prepare a place for you."

Answer: In Matthew 6:19–20, we read: "Do not store up for yourselves treasures on earth, where moth and rust destroy, and where thieves break in and steal. But store up for yourselves treasures in heaven, where moth and rust do not destroy, and where thieves do not break in and steal."

Answer: In Revelations 21:3–4, we read: "And I heard a loud voice from the throne saying, 'Now the dwelling of God is with men, and he will live with them. They will be his people, and God himself will be with them and be their God. He will wipe every tear from their eyes. There will be no more death or mourning or crying or pain, For the old order of things have passed away.'"

Answer: In Romans 10:9–10, we read: "If you confess with your mouth, 'Jesus is Lord,' and believe in your heart that God raised him from the dead, you will be saved. For it is with your heart that you believe and are justified, and it is with your mouth that you confess and are saved."

Question: What are the two magic words that will take you to heaven if you shout out these two words just once?

Answer: In Romans 10:9, we read: "If you confess with your mouth, 'Jesus is Lord,' and believe in your heart that God raised him from the dead, you will be saved. For it is with your heart that you believe and are justified, and it is with your mouth that you confess and are saved."

Basically, the two words that you need to shout out are *Jesus* and *Lord!* And you also need to believe in your heart that God raised Jesus from the dead to be saved as we read in the above verse from the Bible.

Question: What will happen to those who reject God by refusing to believe in the Gospel of Jesus Christ?

Answer: In Matthew 13:41–42, we read: "The Son of Man will… weed out of his kingdom everything that causes sin and all who do evil. They will throw them into the fiery furnace, where there will be weeping and gnashing of teeth."

Answer: In Revelation 21:8, we read: "But the cowardly, the unbelieving, the vile, the murderers, the sexually immoral, those who practice magic arts, the idolaters, and all liars— their place will be in the fiery lake of burning sulfur."

Question: What was the purpose of God in creating man and freeing the Israelites from slavery in Egypt in the Old Testament? Why did God redeem mankind from its sin by giving His only Son, Jesus Christ, as an atonement for their sin? Answer: In Isaiah 43:20–21, we read: "I chose my people and formed them so that they may proclaim my praise."

Answer: In Exodus 5:1, we read, "Moses and Aaron went to Pharaoh and said, 'This is what the Lord, the God of Israel, says: 'Let my people go, so that they may hold a festival to me in the desert'.'"

Answer: In Romans 12–1, we read: "Therefore, I urge you, brothers, in view of God's mercy, to offer your bodies as living sacrifices, holy and pleasing to God—this is your spiritual act of worship."

Answer: In 1 Corinthians 6:19–20, we read: "Do you not know that your body is a temple of the Holy Spirit, who is in you, whom you have received from God? You are not your own; you were bought at a price. Therefore, honor God with your body."

Answer: In Colossians 3:17, we read: "And whatever you do, whether in word or deed, do it all in the name of the Lord Jesus, giving thanks to God the Father through him."

Answer: In 1 Peter 2:4–5, we read: "As you come to him, the living stone—rejected by men but chosen by God and precious to him—you also, like living stones, are being built into a spiritual house to be a holy priesthood, offering spiritual sacrifices acceptable to God through Jesus Christ."

So much to gain…at so little cost!

Even more reasons to call on the name of the Lord.

In the Bible, we read about a donkey who was more spiritual than a prophet—the Prophet Balaam! We read about this in Numbers 22:28–33. Here God uses the donkey to advise the Prophet Balaam by opening his inner eyes. In the story, the donkey opposed and prevented the prophet from proceeding on to a reckless path thus saving the prophet's life. Only when the Lord opened Balaam's eyes did he see the angel of the Lord standing in the road with his sword drawn (Num. 22:31).

In Isaiah 43:20–21, we read about God lamenting over the truth that even though He provides water and streams in the desert and wastelands to give water to humans who are His chosen ones. But they do not praise Him. However, the wild animals like the owls and jackals praised him even though they, only as incidental beneficiaries, happened to benefit from such amenities that God meant for His chosen ones, namely mankind. Seeing the contradiction in the logic, which is the fact that the behavior of wild animals, which honors God even though they are only incidental beneficiaries of the water that God provides in the desert on the one side, and on the other side, the humans for whom God created the availability of water but are almost totally oblivious of their blessing which God has given them, God laments over their illogical and unappreciative attitude and behavior. In Isaiah 43:22, God even reprimands the sons of Jacob meaning all of us, who exhibit such ungrateful attitude towards Him.

The Word of God calls our attention to the ungrateful attitude of the people of God in several places in the Word of God such as in Romans 13:11–14 where Paul sternly warns us to wake up from our slumber to lay aside the deeds of darkness and to put on the armor of light. This simply means that we must start doing the right thing even if it means admitting that wild animals are acting more smartly and wisely than we human beings! Lately, the ongoing coronavirus and all other pandemics, which are pestering us and seem to get worse and worse with each passing day, are nothing but the expressions of God's resentment of our continued disregard for His will and His commandments.

Under these circumstances, what we need to do is to call upon His name and beg for His mercy and grace. We need to do this not merely to get rid of the pandemics that are going around and seeming to get worse and more varied, but also to spread the Gospel by which we are to be saved. During the first Pentecost, Peter in his preaching of the Word of God that pertains to how we can be saved quoted Joel 2:32 which says: "Everyone who calls on the name of the Lord will be saved."

At no time in the past have we been in such a desperate need as this that we need to call on the name of the Lord since, apart from the spread of deadly diseases, attacks of Satan against the children of God have never been so fierce that even our spiritual leaders have no clue as to which direction the children of God are to take to make our eternal salvation most assured. When we look around, spiritually speaking, our path has never been so dark and our resources so few!

There is no doubt that we must call on the name of the Lord if we want to ensure our salvation by avoiding the eternal fires of hell! Literally, we are living in such a time that deception is all around us, so much so that what we read in Jeremiah 17:9 is so true: "The heart is deceitful above all things and beyond cure." We need the guidance of the Holy Spirit more than ever. And for this, as Jesus tells us emphatically in John 3:3, we must be born again.

To get this message across the world, we also need a New Pentecost! These are the twin purposes for which this book will be a huge asset to you. And the prayer rallies, which are being planned across the globe, is what will give us the strength that we need to get it all done by the strength and guidance of the Holy Spirit and the mighty grace of the Risen Savior who is our refuge and our rock and our single-focused hope and our eternal peace! I am imploring everyone to join the prayer rallies that will be held in different parts of the world so that we can all call on the name of the Lord and thus be saved by the merits of our Lord Jesus Christ to whom belongs all the glory as He is our Lord, Savior, Redeemer, Refuge, and Ever-Present Help everywhere and at all times! Praise the Lord. Hallelujah!

About the Author

The title The Prophet from Oklahoma City, USA is a God designated title that was conveyed to the author through a Catholic priest, Rev. Jose Vettiyankal, who has been his spiritual mentor for several years. He received this title during an evangelization trip that he accompanied him for and held in Oklahoma City, USA. Ever since he received this title, he has been bearing and proudly using this title to add authenticity to his preaching through the medium of his Facebook ministry that he had for the past eight years or so.

The use of this title has given him a tremendous boost to his confidence that the Lord has been with him all these years, even as he took each and every step during and as part of this FB ministry. He will be remiss if he failed to emphasize the fact that this *prophetic title* has served as a reminder that the Holy Spirit has been providing him the source of his divine inspiration that guided his every step in conducting this ministry as well as in writing this powerful book by "willing and acting according to God's good purpose" (Phil. 2:13).

Therefore, he is confident that the teaching enabled through him by the Spirit's most precious guidance in writing this book will go a long way for "teaching, rebuking, correcting and training in righteousness so that the man of God may be thoroughly equipped for every good work" (2 Tim. 3:16–17).

www.ingramcontent.com/pod-product-compliance
Lightning Source LLC
Chambersburg PA
CBHW061446150726
47987CB00001B/348